An Introduction

Olympic-Style

WEIGHTLIFTING

Second Edition

John M. Cissik, C.S.C.S.
Texas A&M University

The McGraw-Hill Companies, Inc.
Primis Custom Publishing

New York   St. Louis   San Francisco   Auckland   Bogotá
Caracas   Lisbon   London   Madrid   Mexico   Milan   Montreal
New Delhi   Paris   San Juan   Singapore   Sydney   Tokyo   Toronto

An Introduction to Olympic-Style Weightlifting

McGraw-Hill's Primis Custom Series consists of products that are produced from camera-ready copy. Peer review, class testing, and accuracy are primarily the responsibility of the author(s).

67890 QSR QSR 09876543

ISBN 0-07-043488-3

Editor: Sharon Noble
Cover Design: Kurt F. Ciliberto
Printer/Binder: Quebecor Printing Dubuque, Inc.

Table of Contents

Introduction   **page vi**

Acknowledgments   **page vii**

Part One: The Lifts   **page 1**

Chapter One: Safety and General Technique Information   **page 2**

Safety and Injury Prevention   page 2
 Preventing Injuries   page 3
- Proper Footwear   page 3
- Correct Technique   page 3
- Proper Back Management   page 3
- Learn to Miss the Bar   page 4
- Other Safety Precautions   page 5

General Technique of the Olympic Lifts   page 5
 Hold Your Breath   page 5
 Stay Balanced   page 5
 Learn the Exercises in the Proper Order   page 6

Chapter Two: The Clean   **page 8**

The Classic (or Squat) Clean   page 9
Learning the Clean   page 12
 Progression #1   page 12
- Exercises to be Mastered First   page 12
- Progressions for the Clean   page 17
 Progression #2   page 22
- Exercises to be Mastered First   page 22
- Progressions for the Clean   page 23
 Comments on the Progression Types   page 24
 Biomechanical Information on the Clean   page 25

Chapter Three: The Jerk   **page 29**

The Jerk   page 29
Exercises to be Mastered First   page 32
- Military Press   page 32
Progressions for the Jerk   page 33
- Push Jerk   page 33
- Squat Jerk   page 34
Biomechanical Information on the Jerk   page 35

Chapter Four: The Snatch   page   38
The Classic (or Squat) Snatch   page   38
Determining Grip Width for the Snatch   page   41
Learning the Snatch   page   43
  Progression #1   page   43
  • Exercises to be Mastered First   page   43
  • Progressions for the Power Snatch   page   44
  • Progressions for Squatting with the Barbell Overhead   page   49
  Progression #2   page   52
Comments on Different Progressions   page   55
Biomechanical Information on the Snatch   page   55

Chapter Five: Assistance Exercises   page   58
Squats   page   58
Bend Overs   page   58
  • Good Mornings   page   59
  • Romanian Deadlifts   page   62
Pulls   page   63
Clean Assistance Exercises   page   65
Jerk Assistance Exercises   page   66
Snatch Assistance Exercises   page   66
Olympic Lifting and the Bench Press   page   67

Part Two: Program Design and Periodization   page   68

Chapter Six: General Program Design   page   69
Terms   page   69
Exercise Categories   page   71
Misc. Program Design Notes   page   72
Periodization Basics   page   73
Warming Up and Flexibility   page   74

Chapter Seven: Program Design for Beginners   page   77
What is a beginner?   Page   77
How the training year is broken down   page   78
The First Macrocycle   page   78
  • Transitional Mesocycle   page   79
  • General Preparation Mesocycle   page   80
  • Special Preparation Mesocycle   page   83
  • Competition Mesocycles   page   87
The Second Macrocycle   page   91
The Third Macrocycle   page   92
  • Transitional Mesocycle   page   92
  • General Preparation Mesocycle   page   94
  • Special Preparation Mesocycle   page   94
  • Competition Mesocycles   page   95

Chapter Eight: Program Design for Intermediates   **page 98**
What is an intermediate?   page 98
How the training year is broken down   page 98
The First Macrocycle   page 99
- Transitional Mesocycle   page 99
- General Preparation Mesocycle   page 100
- Special Preparation Mesocycle   page 103
- Competition Mesocycles   page 108
The Second Macrocycle   page 112
The Third Macrocycle   page 113
- Transitional Mesocycle   page 113
- General Preparation Mesocycle   page 114
- Special Preparation Mesocycle   page 115
- Competition Mesocycles   page 116

Part Three: Common Errors   **page 118**

Chapter Nine: Common Errors With The Clean   **page 119**
Starting Position Errors   page 119
Pull Errors   page 120
Receiving Errors   page 121

Chapter Ten: Common Errors With The Jerk   **page 123**
Errors during the dip and drive   page 123
Errors during the split   page 124
Errors during the recovery   page 125

Chapter Eleven: Common Errors With The Snatch   **page 126**
Starting Position Errors   page 126
Pull Errors   page 127
Receiving Errors   page 127

Appendix: Weight Classes and IWF Competition Rules **page 130**
Weight Classes   page 130
IWF Competition Rules   page 130

Introduction

This book has gone through a lot of changes since it's 1st edition. Many of the pictures have been changed, new exercises have been added and other exercises have been dropped. I also decided to use two elite lifters to demonstrate the competition movements - since their technique is excellent.

I have reorganized a number of the chapters to make them more logical (at least in my mind). I am breaking somewhat with USA Weightlifting's Club Coach way of doing things and presenting alternative methods to learning the various exercises.

The program design section has been completely rewritten. This book is written to be a textbook in a college course, so its primary audience is college-age lifters. As a result of this, the program design section is designed around collegiate competitions. This needs to be taken into account when reading that section of the book, as lifters from different stages of life will have different training needs.

I see this book as a work permanently in progress. Parts of this book will change as my experience and knowledge changes. I find that I have to continually question, learn, and forget things that I thought I knew as I proceed with coaching and lifting. It keeps life interesting!

Acknowledgments

A number of people helped with this book. First I'd like to give a big thank you to Ursula Kechko and Stacey Ketchum. Both were good sports about letting me use them for the pictures of the competition lifts - especially since the pictures were taken right after a meet. This was also my chance to give a little back to Ursula (sorry, the flash didn't go off - could you hold that position a little longer?).

I also wanted to thank the people that looked over this manuscript and helped me out - after all, I knew what I meant to say, but could anyone else figure it out? Steve Plisk, MS, CSCS (Yale University) and Grover Furr III, Ph.D. (Montclair State University) both looked at parts of the manuscript and offered some valuable insights.

My students from the spring of 1998 are in many of the newer pictures in this 2nd edition. They were good sports and I've found that it's fun to involve them in this process.

Two people from Texas A&M University deserve special mention, as they both have a great ability to motivate you to work hard - Ernie Kirkham and Robert Armstrong, Ph.D.

Finally, I want to thank Ewa. I promise that this will be the last book you have to look over for a while! Well, maybe...

PART ONE: THE LIFTS

This section of the book is meant to provide the reader with the information they need to learn the lifts. This part of the book draws heavily from USA Weightlifting's Club Coach approach to learning the lifts; however it also presents alternatives to that style of learning. Both approaches presented in this section have their strengths and weaknesses.

Chapter One
Safety and General Technique Information

Chapter Outline:

Safety and Injury Prevention
  Preventing Injuries
    Proper Footwear
    Correct Technique
    Proper Back Management
    Learn to Miss the Bar
    Other Safety Precautions
      No horseplay

Take care of hands
Progress slowly
General Technique of the Olympic Lifts
  Hold Your Breath
  Stay Balanced
  Learn the Exercises in the Proper Order

Chapter Objectives:

1. Understand the importance of correct footwear for safety and balance
2. Understand the importance of correct technique for preventing injuries
3. Understand the back posture that is used in the Olympic lifts and why
4. Understand the concept of center of gravity and how it applies to Olympic lifting
5. Understand how and why to miss the bar
6. Understand when, how, and why to hold the breath during lifting
7. Be familiar with the body's center of gravity when lifting
8. Understand why it is important to learn the exercises in the proper progressions

Safety and Injury Prevention

Because weightlifting is a fast, explosive activity that involves deep squats, stretching, and occasionally missing the bar, weightlifters can be at risk to severe injury if proper technique isn't observed (8).

Many of the injuries that are associated with weightlifting are due to two things: poor technique and stupid accidents (6). Risser (1990) and Zemper (1990) both looked into injuries associated with lifting weights. While they did not specifically investigate Olympic-style weightlifting, their information bears looking at nevertheless. Looking at the information that they present leads to the conclusion that good technique is extremely important to the prevention of injuries. For example, Zemper reveals that 40% of the reported injuries from the weight room for a little over ten thousand college football players were low-back injuries - i.e. "technique-related" injuries (19, pg. 33). In addition, an uncluttered lifting environment is important for safety. Equipment should not be left around that lifters can trip over!

By taking certain precautions one can insure that weightlifting is a safe sport. This section discusses how to prevent injuries in weightlifting.

Preventing Injuries

What follows are things you can do to prevent injuries in weightlifting. Basically, there are several areas you should pay attention to:
1. Use proper footwear
2. Use correct technique
3. Learn proper back management
4. Learn to miss the bar
5. Miscellaneous safety precautions

Choose Proper Footwear

When lifting weights you should wear a closed toe shoe (i.e. no sandals or bare feet). This helps to protect your feet if anything is dropped on them. If you are planning to become competitive in weightlifting, then weightlifting shoes are highly recommended. These shoes help to keep you balanced, flat-footed, and keep you from sinking into your shoes during a heavy overhead lift (17).

Use Correct Technique

Incorrect lifting technique will place your body in positions that exert enormous strains and imbalances on the muscles and connective tissues (17). Incorrect technique can lead to strains and sprains of tendons and ligaments and can also cause chronic overuse injuries such as tendinitis, stress fractures, bursitis, etc. (5, 16).

Learn Proper Back Management

The Olympic lifts provide a large load to the lumbar spine, as Conroy, et al (1993), demonstrate in their examination of the bone mineral density at the lumbar spine of 25 elite adolescent Olympic lifters. They found that the lifters had a marked increase in bone mineral density at the lumbar spine when compared even to 20-39 year old men (7). If there is enough compression that the bone must adapt, then there is enough compression to possibly cause injury if the lifts are done improperly. To help safeguard against this, during all parts of the Olympic lifts an arched back posture is used. This helps the body to effectively transmit force from the legs and hips to the bar and it prevents collapse and loss of balance during the exercises (17).

According to Zatsiorsky, "When the body is inclined forward, the activity of muscles that extend the spinal column increases at first, then with a deeper lean this activity almost completely disappears." This means that when the back is not arched, the muscles do not assume the load, the ligaments and the fasciae of the back do. As a result, pressure on the inter-vertebral disks is high when an arched back is not used (18). In addition, the arched back will aid in preventing collapse and loss of balance in the receiving phases of the snatch, clean, and jerk (10, 17). This posture is referred to in this book as *setting the back*.

Figure 1-1 demonstrates the load on the intervertebral disks when 50 kg is lifted by different methods. This figure shows that when the movement is lifted by an arched back (the right hand figure) then the compression loads on the intervertebral disks are lower than when lifting with a rounded back. In addition, when lifting with an arched back the compressive forces are distributed better around the intervertebral disk.

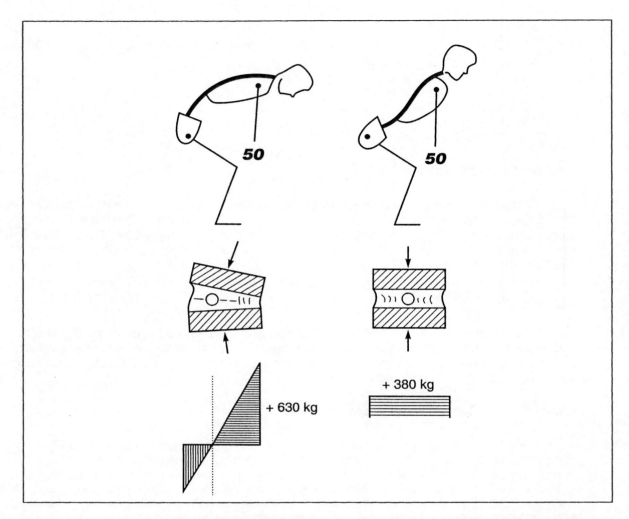

Figure 1-1: Load on the intervertebral disks when 50kg is lifted by different methods. From Zatsiorsky, V.M. (1994). <u>Science and Practice of Strength Training.</u> Champaign, Il: Human Kinetics, 190. Reprinted by permission of V.M. Zatsiorsky.

Learn to Miss the Bar

When performing the Olympic lifts, the objective is to lift as much weight as possible from the floor to a position overhead. When a weight is overhead, the body's area of balance is the area from the heel to the toe of the shoes, across the width of foot placement. In other words, there is a box around the feet that the bar should be kept over. This is also known as the *center of gravity*. If the barbell, elbows, shoulders, and hips of the lifter is kept over this area, the lifter will have control over the bar (3).

During the Olympic lifts, spotters are not recommended (2). This is because from day one weightlifters should be taught how to miss the bar correctly. This is a critical skill to master because there are no spotters in a competition (4).

Fortunately, the weight plates are made of rubber - so they bounce when dropped on the floor. When a lift is missed, because the weight is too heavy or because technique is bad (i.e. when, for whatever reason the barbell is not kept over the center of gravity), the bar should be dropped and the lifter should get out of the way.

When an overhead weight is caught too far behind, causing you to be off-balance, the weight should be dropped behind while stepping forward. When the bar is caught too far in front, the bar should be dropped in front as you step back (2, 4).

Failure to miss an overhead lift correctly can lead to serious injury (3).

Some other safety precautions presented by Lyn Jones include (11):
1. No horseplay - be aware of other lifters in the vicinity. If you are not lifting, you should stay off the platform.
2. Take care of your hands- calluses should be filed down to insure that they don't rip off while lifting.
3. Make sure that you progress slowly- don't try to make big jumps. Trying to lift too heavy too early can lead to injury and bad technique.

General Techniques of the Olympic Lifts

The olympic lifts are performed very rapidly in competition. In elite international competition, the major lifting forces are applied to the bar for only about .8 seconds in the snatch and clean, and .2 seconds in the jerk (9). Because the lifts occur so quickly, technique is critical. According to Roman: "The exercises need to be executed as precisely as possible, this insures that the bar's trajectory is optimal and the force the athlete develops will be utilized to the maximum" (15). In Olympic lifting, technique *always* limits the amount of weight lifted (10, 11). Before getting into the specifics of each exercise, here are some general guidelines for the olympic lifts:

Hold Your Breath

Believe it or not, it is important to hold your breath while performing the olympic lifts - especially during max attempts. Holding your breath will result in the chest being inflated; this causes the lungs to act as a brace on the back. In other words, by holding your breath you help to keep the back from rounding during the lift (11).

However, caution should be taken. While you should hold your breath during each lift - you should not hold your breath during an entire set. In other words, it is okay to hold your breath during each *repetition*. After each repetition you should take the time to exhale and inhale before lifting the bar again. Also, you should avoid inspiring maximally before a lift because this can unnecessarily increase intra-thoracic pressure (18). Care must be taken to insure that holding one's breath while lifting is done properly. Failure to do so can lead to serious health problems such as fainting (while lifting) or even possibly something as severe as a pneumo-thorax (12).

Stay Balanced

It is important to stay balanced, especially when the bar is overhead. When the barbell is overhead the bar and the lifter have a combined center of gravity and this center of gravity is closest to the heavier body (11).   This is important to know because it means that as the weight on the bar changes, the center of gravity will also change. In other words, the exercises are essentially different when performed with different weights on the bar (15). For this reason, the bar should be kept over the box that is from the heel to the toes and across the width of the foot placement (see the section on safety for more about this).

Learn the Exercises in the Proper Order

When teaching any movement-related skill, proper progression is essential to mastering that skill (1). In Olympic lifting, the exercises are taught from the top down. Lifts are taught from a standing position with the bar at above the knee level initially. Then as the lifter masters that position, he/she starts from lower and lower positions - until the lifter is starting with the bar on the platform (11, 13). This takes what is essentially a complicated movement skill and makes it simpler to learn - allowing people to experience success as they attempt to learn the lifts. It also reinforces good technique.

References

1. Armitage-Johnson, S. (1994). Two assisting exercises for teaching the power clean and power snatch. Strength and Conditioning, 16(4), 51-55.
2. Baechle, T.R., R.W. Earle, & W.B. Allerheiligen. (1994). Strength training and spotting techniques. In Baechle, T.R. (ed.) Essentials of Strength Training and Conditioning (pp. 345-349). Champaign, Il: Human Kinetics.
3. Baker, G. (1994). Safety considerations in teaching the overhead lifts. Strength and Conditioning, 16(1), 40-43.
4. Burgener, M. (1991). How to properly miss with a barbell. NSCA Journal, 13(3), 24-25.
5. Cioroslan, D. (1994). Ask the national coach. Weightlifting U.S.A., 12(3), 4-5.
6. Cissik, J.M. (1998). The Basics of Strength Training. New York: The McGraw-Hill Companies, Primis Custom Publishing, 14-17.
7. Conroy, B.P., W.J. Kraemer, C.M. Maresh, S.J. Fleck, M.H. Stone, A.C. Fry, P.D. Miller, & G.P. Dalsky. (1993). Bone mineral density in elite junior Olympic weightlifters. Medicine and Science in Sports and Exercise, 25(10), 1103-1109.
8. Fitgerald, B., & G.R. McLatchie. (1980). Degenerative joint disease in weight-lifters fact or fiction? British Journal of Sports Medicine, 14, 97-101.
9. Garhammer, J., & B. Takano. (1992). Training for weightlifting. In Komi, P.V. (ed.) Strength and Power in Sport (pp. 357-369). International Olympic Committee.
10. Hamill, B. (1985). Teaching the power clean and power snatch. NSCA Journal, 7(4), 62-65.
11. Jones, L. (1991). USWF Coaching Accreditation Course Club Coach Manual. Colorado Springs, CO: U.S. Weightlifting Federation, 7-12, 33-40.
12. Marnejon, T., S. Sarac, & A.J. Cropp. (1995). Spontaneous pneumothorax in weightlifters. The Journal of Sports Medicine and Physical Fitness, 35, 124-126.
13. Medvedyev, A.S. (1986). A System of Multi-Year Training in Weightlifting. Moscow: Fizkultura i Sport. Translated by Charniga, Jr., A. (1989). Livonia, Michigan: Sportivny Press, 79.
14. Risser, W. L. (1990). Musculoskeletal injuries caused by weight training. Clinical Pediatrics, 29(6), 305-310.
15. Roman, R.A. (1986). The Training of the Weightlifter. Moscow: Fizkultura i Spovt. Translated by Charniga, Jr., A. (1988). Livonia, Michigan: Sportivny Press , 1,40.

16. Stone, M.H., A.C. Fry, M. Ritchie, L. Stoessel-Ross, & J.L. Marsit. (1994). Injury potential and safety aspects of weightlifting movements. <u>Strength and Conditioning, 16</u>(3), 15-21.

17. Takano, B. (1987). Coaching optimal technique in the clean and jerk, Part I. <u>NSCA Journal, 9</u>(5), 50-59.

18. Zatsiorsky, V.M. (1994). <u>Science and Practice of Strength Training.</u> Champaign, Il: Human Kinetics, 169-171, 188-192.

19. Zemper, E. D. (1990). Four-year study of weightroom injuries in a national sample of college football teams. <u>NSCA Journal, 12</u>(3), 32-34.

Chapter Two
The Clean

Chapter Outline:

The Classic (or Squat) Clean
Learning the Clean
  Progression #1
    Exercises to be Mastered First
      The Back Squat
      The Front Squat
      The Jumping with the Bar Exercise
    Progressions for the Clean
      The Hang Power Clean from Above
      the Knees
      The Hang Power Clean from Below
      the Knees
      The Power Clean
  Progression #2

    Exercises to be Mastered First
      The Back Squat
      The Front Squat
      The Clean-Grip Deadlift
    Progressions for the Clean
      Deadlift + Shrug
      Deadlift + Jump
      Power Clean
      Power Clean + Front Squat
Comments on the Progression Types
Biomechanical Information on the
Clean

Chapter Objectives:

1. Understand how the clean is performed
2. Be familiar with the two different progressions for learning the clean
3. Understand the correct ways to perform the exercises that should be mastered before attempting to learn the clean
4. Understand how and why to perform each of the progressions for the clean and what the differences are between the various exercises

The clean is the first half of the clean and jerk; this is the second lift performed in competition. In America it is usually taught to lifters first because it is easier to master than the other lifts. This lift is also widely used in athletics to improve explosive power.

This chapter will present the techniques for performing the classic (a.k.a. squat) clean. To go with the idea of progressions mentioned in the last section, certain exercises should be mastered before beginning to learn the clean. These exercises will familiarize you with keeping the back in proper position, with learning when and how to hold your breath safely during lifting, with balancing the bar on the front of the shoulders during a squat, and finally they will help you learn how to be explosive. This chapter will describe two different progressions that can be used for learning the clean - with each exercise being broken down and described. Each progression has its strengths and weaknesses, as will be discussed later.

Classic (or Squat) Clean

Purpose of the exercise: This is the competition lift. It is the second lift that is performed in competition.

Starting position:
1. The bar is on the floor.
2. The feet are approximately hip-width apart.
3. Have the bar resting against the shins.
4. Squat down, putting the stomach between the legs.
5. Grip the bar slightly wider than shoulder-width apart.
6. Take a deep breath, hold it, then set the back.
7. The shoulders should be slightly in front of the bar and the elbows should be rotated out (7, 9, 19).
8. The hips should be higher than the knees in this position (see photo 2-1).

Photo 2-1: The starting position of the clean.

Photo 2-2: The first pull of the clean.

First pull:
1. The first pull refers to the period of the lift where the bar is brought from the floor to the level of the knees.

> The first pull is done is a slow, controlled manner. There are several reasons for this; first, if the first pull is done too quickly, the amount of force the lifter can generate in overcoming the bar's inertia will decrease - because as velocity increases force production decreases (19). Second, generating excessive speed off the floor will result in pulling with a bent back, inappropriate elevation of the hips, and the making of other "tiny" mistakes that can result in missing the lift later on (10, 17). In other words, the bar should not be ripped off the floor during the first pull!

2. The first pull is achieved by extending the knees. As the knees extend, the bar

should move back towards you (app. 40-70mm) (10). During the first pull care must be taken to keep the back set (see photo 2-2).

Photo 2-4: The second pull of the clean.

Photo 2-3: Scraping the thighs during the clean.

Second pull:
1. Once the bar has reached knee height, the second pull begins. This is the explosive part of the lift.
2. When the bar reaches knee level, continue to extend the knees until the bar scrapes your thighs (see photo 2-3).
3. Once the bar scrapes your thighs, extend your hips violently and jump up while shrugging your shoulder girdle up. Your shoulders and your hips should move at the same speed during both the first and second pulls (1) (see photo 2-4).

> Note: The knee then hip activation pattern that is the first and second pulls may actually be highly important. There is some evidence to indicate that this sequential activation of the knee and hip joints may be necessary to achieve the maximal rate of speed during lifting (16).

Nonsupport phase:
1. This is the period of time when your feet are not in contact with the ground.
2. When jumping off of the ground during the second pull, you should be preparing to land with the feet wider than when they started. This is necessary to allow you to land in a deep squat.

Photo 2-5: The amortization phase of the clean.

Amortization phase:
1. Land on the ground with your feet slightly wider than hip-width apart, in other words your feet will be slightly wider than they were when the exercise started.
2. Ideally, when landing on the ground the bar should be caught in the deep squat position (see photo 2-5).
3. Your back should be set and your elbows should be high.

4. Caution should be taken here. More is not better. Your feet should be slightly wider than hip-width apart. Many lifters get in the habit of spreading their feet too wide. This slows a person down and makes the lift inefficient. It can also lead to knee injuries.

End position:
1. From the squat position, straighten up until you are standing up - back set, elbows high, bar on the shoulders (see photo 2-6).
2. From here you will go into the jerk.

Photo 2-6: The end position of the clean.

Things to remember:
1. Speed of movement is critical to the squat clean.
2. One important thing to remember is that while your feet need to split to the side during this exercise, be careful not to overdo that split (i.e. more is not better). If your feet are split too wide, this can cause knee problems over time.
3. Your back must be set throughout the exercise, otherwise you will have no control over the bar when catching it in the deep squat position. One of the major reasons that people "miss" a clean is due to the fact that they slump forward while in the squat, losing control of the barbell.
4. Finally, remember that if the elbows touch any part of the thighs during the squat clean, this will disqualify the lift!

Common Errors: Some of the more common errors associated with the squat clean are:
1. Failure to "land" on flat feet
2. Hitting the knees instead of scraping the thighs
3. Throwing the bar away from the body
4. Bending the elbows during the first and second pulls
5. Losing control of the bar when racking it

These errors are discussed in detail in chapter nine.

Progression #1 for learning the clean

This progression has two parts. The first consists of those exercises that should be mastered before attempting the other exercises. These are important because each of the exercises teaches fundamental skills. Once those exercises are mastered the lifter should move to the progressions for the actual clean.

The exercises that should be mastered first are:
1. The back squat
2. The front squat
3. The jumping with the bar exercise

The Back Squat

Purpose of the exercise: This exercise is used to develop strength in the legs and hips. It is the basis of all weightlifting programs (1, 7). This exercise also helps to teach proper back management, balance, and how to breath properly.

Photo 2-7: The starting position of the back squat.

Starting position:
1. Grasp the bar with a grip that is slightly wider than shoulder-width.
2. Set the bar on the back so that it is high on the shoulders or upper back.
3. Step away from the squat rack and place the feet approximately shoulder-width apart.
4. Take a deep breath (to inflate the chest) and hold it.
5. Set the back so that the chest is high and the shoulders are back (all the muscles running along the spine should tense up) (see photo 2-7).

Photo 2-8: The bottom position of the back squat.

The squat:
1. From the starting position, squat down so that your stomach is placed between your legs.
2. Squat down as far as possible with your feet flat on the floor (1, 7).

3. *All squatting movements should be initiated by the hips, not the knees.* When squatting, your hips should initially move back and down. The knees should then follow (see photo 2-8).

End position:
1. From the bottom position, straighten the legs.
2. Once standing back up, let out the breath, take another one, reset the back, and squat again (1, 7).

Things to remember:
1. Remember to keep your back set throughout the exercise, on the way down and the way up.
2. It is very important to keep your feet flat on the floor throughout the exercise; failure to do so can result in excessive pressure on the knees.
3. In addition it is also important that the hips start all squatting movements. If the knees are allowed to move too far in front of the toes, this can result in excessive wear and tear on the knees.

Common Errors: Some of the more common errors associated with the back squat are:
1. Failure to keep the back set during the squat - Usually lifters do a good job of setting the back at the beginning of a lift. However, it must be stressed that a lifter should keep their back set throughout the entire lift. This is important to do with deep squats as it will keep an excessive amount of pressure off the low back.
2. Failure to keep the feet flat on the floor during the squat - When first starting out, some lifters are unable to squat down deeply with their feet flat on the floor. This is typically due to two things. First, they may not be using their hips to initiate the squat. If lifters start the squat by bending their knees, instead of moving their hips back and down, they will not be able to keep their feet flat on the floor. Second, this can be an ankle flexibility problem. If this is the case, then lifters should only squat down as far as they can *while keeping their feet flat on the floor*.

The Front Squat

Purpose of the exercise: This exercise also strengthens the muscles of the legs and hips. In addition it teaches you to balance the bar on the front of the shoulders. The bottom position of the front squat is the receiving position during the squat clean, so this is a critical exercise to become comfortable with (7).

Starting position:
1. The bar is gripped with a shoulder– width grip.
2. Place your shoulders under the bar and push your elbows upward and inward. This will place the bar on the shoulders.
3. Step back from the squat rack.
4. Take a deep breath and hold it.
5. Set the back (this will help to keep the elbows high) (see photo 2-9).

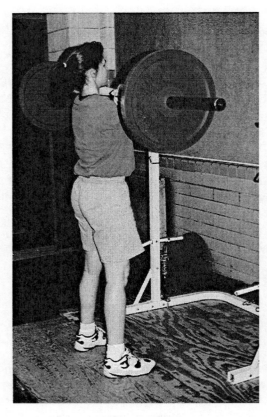

Photo 2-9: The starting position of the front squat.

Photo 2-10: The bottom position of the front squat.

The squat:
1. Once the back is set and the elbows are high, squat down as deeply as possible - trying to put your stomach between the legs.
2. Keep an upright trunk during this exercise (1, 7).
3. Once again, all squatting movements should be initiated by the hips, not the knees. When squatting, the hips should initially move back and down. The knees should then follow (see photo 2-10).

End position:
1. From the squat straighten the legs.
2. Once standing up, let out the breath, take another, reset the back, and squat again.

Things to remember:
1. It is critical to keep the back set on this exercise; this will keep the elbows high. If the elbows are allowed to drop, or if you for any reason slump forward, you will lose control of the bar.
2. An upright trunk is important to keeping control of the bar.
3. For the same reason, the feet must remain flat on the floor during this exercise.

Common Errors: Some of the more common errors associated with the front squat are:
1. Failure to keep the back set during the squat
2. Failure to keep the feet flat on the floor during the squat
3. Failure to keep the elbows high during the squat - This error is usually due to one of two things. First, the lifter may not be setting their back or keeping their back set during the exercise. Allowing the shoulders to slump forward will cause the elbows to drop, making the bar more difficult to control. A second cause has to do with the way the bar is gripped. Many people do not have the wrist flexibility to grip the bar tightly and keep their elbows high. As a result, lifters are encouraged to keep their hands open when performing this exercise. If the elbows are kept high, and the back is set, then the bar will not move anywhere. This will also reduce some of the pressure on the wrists.
4. Wrist pain during the front squat - This is a common problem. It can result from several things: grip width, lack of flexibility, or disuse. If the grip is too wide, this can lead to the lifter having the bar rest on their hands instead of on their shoulders, which will result in the wrist supporting all the weight (instead of the shoulders).

Photo 2-11: Starting position for the jumping with the bar exercise.

Jumping with the Bar

Purpose of the exercise: This exercise is designed to teach how to explode with the barbell. Unlike the back and front squats, this is not a conditioning exercise and should be discontinued after it has been mastered.

Starting position:
1. Pick up the bar, with the same grip width used on the front squat.
2. Upon standing up, take a deep breath and hold it.
3. Set the back.
4. From this position, bend forward *from the hips* until the bar is touching the thigh at about mid-thigh level. It is important to get there by bending the hips - not by squatting down.
5. The feet should be hip-width apart (see photo 2-11).

Explosion:
1. From that position, which is also known as a hang with the bar above the knee, jump straight up in the air with the bar in the hands.
2. When jumping, two things should happen at the same time; you should keep your arms straight, and you should shrug your shoulders up violently at the same time you jump off the ground (2). This action will cause the barbell to move up the body (see photo 2-4).

End position:
1. When landing, the feet should be in the same place they started from. In other words, you should jump straight up - not backwards or forwards.
2. Avoid splitting the feet to either side when jumping.

Things to remember:
1. Remember to use the entire body to jump with the bar (i.e. pull with the shoulders when jumping off the floor).
2. Keep the back set throughout the exercise.
3. Make sure that you jump straight up - not forward or backward.
4. Remember to keep the bar close to the body during the lift. The bar should not be pushed away while jumping up. If the bar is not kept close to the body during these exercises, it makes the movements harder to perform.

Once those three exercises are mastered, the lifter is ready to begin learning the clean. The progressions for the clean are as follows (7, 10):
1. Hang Power Clean from Above the Knees
2. Hang Power Clean from Below the Knees
3. Power Clean
4. Squat Clean

Hang Power Clean from Above the Knees

Purpose of the exercise: This exercise continues to teach you how to explode, but it also teaches you to catch the bar on the front of the shoulders.

Starting position:
1. The starting position is the same as in the jump with the bar exercise.
2. Bend forward from your hips and hold the bar at thigh level.
3. Remember to hold your breath and set your back at the beginning of the exercise (1, 7) (see photo 2-11).

The explosion:
1. From the starting position, jump straight up in the air - as in the jump with the bar exercise. Let the bar travel up your body (see photo 2-4).

Photo 2-12: End position for the hang power clean from above the knees.

End position:
1. At the same time you land on the ground, the bar should be caught on the front of your shoulders.
2. Rebend your knees upon landing to help absorb the force of the impact.
3. When catching the bar on the shoulders, keep the back set and the elbows high (just like in the front squat) (1, 7, 18).
4. When landing, your feet should still be only hip-width apart (i.e. do not split your feet to the sides during this exercise) (see photo 2-12).

Things to remember:
1. In the starting position, it is important to get there by bending at your hips - not by squatting down.
2. It is important to keep the back set throughout the exercise- this not only helps protect the back, but makes controlling the bar easier.
3. Catch the bar with your elbows high and with your back set.
4. Keep the bar close to your body during the entire exercise- if the bar gets away from your body then it becomes harder to control.
5. Speed is critical to making this exercise successful. If the explosion is done slowly, or if it is muscled, you will be limited in how much weight you can use on this exercise. When exploding from the hang position, remember to keep the arms locked. Excessive bending of the elbows will cause the bar to slow down - which will make the exercise harder.

Common Errors: Some of the more common errors associated with the hang power clean from above the knees are:
1. The lifter "squats" into position instead of bending forward from the hips

2. Splitting the feet to the side during hang or power cleans
3. Failure to "land" on flat feet
4. Throwing the bar away from the body

These errors are discussed in detail in chapter nine.

Hang Power Clean from Below the Knees

Purpose of the exercise: This lift is meant to teach you to move the bar around your knees (1). This is often the most difficult progression to learn.

Photo 2-13: Starting position for the hang power clean from below the knees.

Starting position:
1. Stand up with the bar in your hands.
2. Take a deep breath and set your back.
3. Bend forward from your hips until the bar is touching mid-thigh.
4. Then bend at the knees until the bar is lower than your knees.
5. Your shoulders should still be in front of the bar (1, 7) (see photo 2-13).

The explosion:
1. The explosion is much the same as in the previous exercise.
2. First your knees are extended while the bar is brought back towards your body.
3. The bar should scrape your thighs. Then you will jump up and pull with the shoulder girdle (1, 7) (see photos 2-3 and 2-4).

End position:
1. The bar should be caught in the same position as in the previous exercises.
2. Keep your back set and your elbows high.

Things to remember:
1. The knees must be extended first; this will bring the bar back towards your body.
2. Scrape the thighs with the bar because this will help to keep the bar close to your body during the lift.

Common Errors: Some of the more common errors associated with the hang power clean from below the knees are:
1. The lifter "squats" into position instead of bending forward from the hips
2. Splitting the feet to the side during hang or power cleans
3. Failure to "land" on flat feet

4. Hitting the knees instead of scraping the thighs
5. Throwing the bar away from the body

These errors are discussed in detail in chapter nine.

Power Clean

Purpose of the exercise: This exercise teaches you to lift the barbell from the floor. It is also a great conditioning exercise - not only for weightlifters but also for all types of athletes.

Starting position:
1. The bar is on the floor.
2. The feet are approximately hip-width apart.
3. Have the bar resting against the shins.
4. Squat down, putting your stomach between your legs.
5. Grip the bar slightly wider than shoulder-width apart.
6. Take a deep breath, hold it, then set your back.
7. Your shoulders should be slightly in front of the bar and your elbows should be rotated out (7, 9, 10).
8. Your hips should be higher than your knees in this position (see photo 2-1).

First pull:
1. The first pull refers to the period of the lift where the bar is brought from the floor to the level of the knees.
2. The first pull is done is a slow, controlled manner.
3. The first pull is achieved by extending your knees. During the first pull care must be taken to keep your back set (see photo 2-2).

Second pull:
1. Once the bar has reached knee height, the second pull begins. This is the explosive part of the lift.
2. When the bar reaches knee level, continue to extend the knees until the bar scrapes your thighs.
3. Once the bar scrapes the thighs, extend your hips violently and jump up while shrugging the shoulder girdle up. Your shoulders and hips should move at the same speed during both the first and second pulls (1) (see photo 2-3 and 2-4).

Nonsupport phase:
1. The nonsupport phase refers to the period of time during which your feet are not in contact with the ground. Obviously as the weight on the bar increases, the amount of time spent in the nonsupport phase will decrease.

Photo 2-14: Amortization phase of the power clean.

Amortization phase:
1. This is also known as the shock absorbing phase. This is the period of time from when one lands, until they have "caught" the bar with the knees slightly bent.
2. It is important to point out that in the power clean (and in all the clean progressions), when landing your feet should be in roughly the same spot they started from. In other words, your feet should not split forward and backward or to the side. Simply jump straight up into the air (see photo 2-14).

End position:
1. After the amortization phase, you will be in a partial squat.
2. The bar will be on the front of your shoulders, your elbows will be high, and your back will be set.
3. From this position, extend your legs until you are standing straight up.

Things to Remember:
1. Speed is very important during this exercise. If this exercise is performed slowly, or if the bar is muscled, then the exercise will not be very effective.
2. Remember to keep the back set at all times.
3. Slow, controlled knee extension powers the first pull.
4. Violent hip extension and shoulder girdle elevation powers the second pull.
5. The hips and shoulders should travel at the same speed throughout the movement.
6. Also, keep the bar close to your body!

Common Errors: Some of the more common errors associated with the power clean are:
1. Splitting the feet to the side during hang or power cleans
2. Failure to "land" on flat feet
3. Hitting the knees instead of scraping the thighs
4. Throwing the bar away from the body
5. Bending the elbows during the first and second pulls
6. Losing control of the bar when racking it

These errors are discussed in detail in chapter nine.

Progression #2 for learning the clean

Like the first progression, this one involves exercises that should be mastered first before moving on to the other exercises. The exercises that should be mastered first are:
1. The Back Squat
2. The Front Squat
3. Deadlift with a Clean Grip

Deadlift, Clean Grip

Purpose of the Exercise: Essentially, this exercise teaches the first pull of the clean. It is also useful in conditioning the muscles of the lower body and back that are responsible for moving the bar during the first pull.

Starting Position:
1. The bar is on the floor.
2. The feet are approximately hip-width apart.
3. Have the bar resting against the shins.
4. Squat down, putting your stomach between your legs.
5. Grip the bar slightly wider than shoulder-width apart.
6. Take a deep breath, hold it, then set your back.
7. Your shoulders should be slightly in front of the bar and your elbows should be rotated out.
8. Your hips should be higher than your knees in this position (see photo 2-1).

Ending Position:
1. From the starting position extend your legs so that the bar is raised off the ground.
2. Continue to drive with your legs until the bar touches your leg at mid-thigh level (see photo 2-3).
3. Make sure to keep your back set as your pick the bar up.
4. Note that your shoulders and hips should travel up at the same speed.
5. Once the bar has reached mid-thigh level, lower it to the ground for another repetition.

Things to Remember:
1. This should be a slow and controlled exercise. Technique is extremely important on this exercise.

Common Errors:
1. Having the hips travel up faster than the shoulders - This is an inefficient way to lift the bar and results in more strain on the lower back
2. Loss of back set while lifting

Once those exercises have been mastered you are ready to move on to the progressions for learning the clean. Those exercises are:
1. Deadlift, clean grip + Shrug
2. Deadlift, clean grip + Jump
3. Power Clean
4. Power Clean + Front Squat

Deadlift, clean grip + Shrug

Purpose of the Exercise: This is not a conditioning exercise; it is merely presented to help teach the movement patterns associated with learning the clean. After it has been mastered it should be discontinued.

Starting Position:
1. This exercise has the same starting position as the deadlift.

Deadlift:
1. This part of the exercise is performed just like during the deadlift.

Shrug:
1. Once the bar has reached mid-thigh extend your hips.
2. As your hips extend rise up on your toes and shrug your shoulders up (see photo 2-15).
3. Rising on the toes and shrugging should happen at the same time.

Photo 2-15: The ending position for the deadlift + shrug.

Things to Remember:
1. Make sure that when you rise up on your toes and shrug that these activities happen at the same time.

Deadlift, clean grip + Jump

Purpose of the Exercise: This is not a conditioning exercise; it is merely presented to help teach the movement patterns associated with learning the clean. After it has been mastered it should be discontinued. This exercise is designed to help teach technique for the first and second pulls.

Starting Position:
1. The starting position is the same as in the deadlift.

Deadlift:
1. Lift the bar until it reaches mid-thigh, just like in the deadlift.

Jump:
1. Once the bar has reached mid-thigh, jump straight up into the air and shrug your shoulders up.
2. The jump and shrug should happen at the same time (see photo 2-4).
3. Remember to jump straight up, not forwards or backwards.

Ending Position:
1. Make sure, when landing, that your feet land in the same place they started from.

Power Clean + Front Squat

This is a combination exercise and is an excellent conditioning exercise as well as a teaching tool. In this exercise the lifter performs a specified number of power cleans. After the last clean has been performed, while the bar is still on the front of the lifter's shoulders, the lifter will perform a number of front squats. This is a very strenuous exercise and is good for reinforcing the importance of keeping the back set and the elbows high.

Comments on the Different Progressions

Both progressions have their strong and weak points. The first progression involves a systematic learning process of all the components of the clean. It probably leads to a more thorough understanding of technique and position. However, the first progression also takes longer to work your way through - some lifters may take months to work through all the progressions.

The second progression has the benefit of speed - lifters can move through it in a matter of days. The principal drawback to this progression is that lifters then to learn to perform the lift in parts: i.e. they learn to pull the bar to their thighs, then they learn to clean the bar from that mid-thigh position. This is a difficult habit to break lifters of and it is also illegal in competition. Coaches and lifters must continually stress the need to blend the parts together when learning the second progression.

Biomechanical Information on the Clean

So what does the clean look like in competition? There is a good amount of data from the old Soviet Union and from America on that subject. Table 2-1 shows data on the amount of time spent in each phase of the lift for several Soviet Union and East German athletes.

Lifter	Off Plat.	1st Pull	2nd Pull	Non Support	Amort.	Squat
Alexeev	0.24	0.4	0.12	0.2	0.16	0.44
Bonk	0.24	0.44	0.16	0.2	0.2	0.44
Kolev		1.05	0.15	0	0.4	0.5
Shary		0.75	0.15	0.11	0.6	0.8
Rigert		0.6	0.12	0.2	0.45	0.73

Table 2-1: Competition Values for the Clean (11,13,14,15)
Data from references 11, 13, 14, and 15 are reprinted by permission from Sports Training Inc.

Table 2-1 shows the amount of time (in seconds) spent in each phase of the lift. The table shows time spent getting the bar off the platform, in the first pull, in the second pull, in the nonsupport phase, in the amortization phase, and in the squat. You can see from the table that the combined first and second pulls generally take between .72 and 1.20 seconds for those lifters. In other words, the lifters are exerting force on the bar (in most cases) for right around a second. The clean happens very quickly in competition!

In addition to spending a small amount of time in each phase of the lift, lifters also move the bar very quickly. Table 2-2 demonstrates how fast some lifters are moving the barbell during the first and second pulls in competition.

Lifter	1st Pull	2nd Pull
Kolev	1.46	1.5
Shary	1.24	1.8
Rigert	1.3	1.65
Kelley	1.07	1.48
Sermanat	1.51	1.38

Table 2-2: Bar speeds in m/sec (12,13,14,15)
Data from references 12 is reprinted by permission from USA Weightlifting. Data from references 13, 14, and 15 are reprinted by permission from Sports Training Inc.

As can be seen from table 2-2, with the exception of one lifter all of the lifters shown have a faster second pull. This is also the point at which the bar achieves its greatest velocity during the clean. John Garhammer reports that in competition, the maximum bar velocity during the clean ranges from 1.37 m/sec to 1.86 m/sec for male lifters (2, 3, 4). Also, Garhammer reports that women lifters achieve bar velocities between 1.48-1.69 m/sec (4, 5).

26

So, we can see from competition results that generally athletes are exerting force on the bar for somewhere around a second. Most athletes have a faster second pull than first.

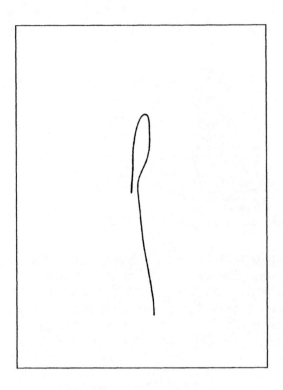

Figure 2-1 Technique of a 180 kg clean. From Jones, L. (1991). <u>USWF Coaching Accreditation Course Senior Coach Manual</u>, Colorado Spring, CO: U.S. Weightlifting Federation, 36, reprinted by permission of USA Weightlifting.

Figure 2-1 shows efficient clean technique. This figure shows the path of the bar when viewed from the side. As can be seen, the bar moves back towards the lifter until the lifter explodes in the second pull. Then as the lifter performs the second pull and begins to drop under the bar it starts to move away from their body (8).

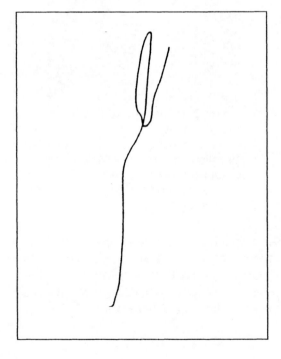

Figure 2-2 Technique of a 175 kg clean. From Jones, L. (1991). <u>USWF Coaching Accreditation Course Senior Coach Manual</u>, Colorado Spring, CO: U.S. Weightlifting Federation, 39, reprinted by permission of USA Weightlifting.

Figure 2-2 shows an inefficient clean technique. This figure shows the lifter moving the bar away from their body during the first and second pulls, causing the lifter to jump forward to catch the bar (9).

References

1. Baker, G. (ed.). (1987). The United States Weightlifting Federation Coaching Manual Volume I Technique. Colorado Springs, CO: U.S.Weightlifting Federation,. 35, 36, 61-67.

2. Garhammer, J. (1981). Biomechanical characteristics of the 1978 world weight-lifting champions. In Biomechanics VIIB: Proceedings of the Seventh International Congress of Biomechanics, Warsaw, Poland. Baltimore: University Park Press, 300-304.

3. Garhammer, J. (1985). Biomechanical profiles of Olympic weightlifters. International Journal of Sport Biomechanics, 1, 122-130.

4. Garhammer, J. (1990). Bar trajectories of world champion male and female weight-lifters. International Olympic Lifter, 10(6), 12-13.

5. Garhammer, J. (1991). A comparison of maximal power outputs between elite male and female weightlifters in competition. International Journal of Sport Biomechanics, 7, 3-11.

6. Johnson, J. (1982). Teaching the power clean and the hang power clean. NSCA Journal, 4(4), 52-54.

7. Jones, L. (1991). USWF Coaching Accreditation Course Club Coach Manual. Colorado Springs, CO.: U.S. Weightlifting Federation, 40-43, 47-50, 62.

8. Jones, L. (1991). USWF Coaching Accreditation Course Senior Coach Manual. Colorado Springs, CO.: U.S. Weightlifting Federation, 36, 39.

9. Medvedev, A. (1989). Three periods of the snatch and clean and jerk. NSCA Journal, 10(6), 33-38.

10. Medvedyev, A.S. (1986). A System of Multi-Year Training in Weightlifting. Moscow: Fizkultura i Sport. Translated by Charniga, Jr., A. Livonia, Michigan: Sportivny Press, 53-59, 79.

11. Medvedev, A.S., and Lukashov, A.A. (1977). Jerk technique of world recordholders Alexeev and Bonk. Tyazhelaya Atletika, 1, 60-62. Translated by Yesis, M. (1981). Soviet Sports Review, 16(1), 11-17.

12. Reiser, R., and Cioroslan, D. (1995). Comparative biomechanical analysis of clean technique in competition. Weightlifting U.S.A., 13(4), 6-9.

13. Roman, R.A., and Shakirzyanov, M.S. (1978). Jerk technique analysis: David Rigert. Ryvok I Tolchok. Translated by Yesis, M. (1980). Soviet Sports Review,15(3), 127-132.

14. Roman, R.A., and Shakirzyanov, M.S. (1979). Clean and jerk technique analysis of Valery Shary. Tyazhelaya Atletika, 17-21. Translated by Yesis, M. (1980). Soviet Sports Review, 15(1), 22-28.

15. Roman, R.A., and Shakirzyanov, M.S. (1981). Jerk technique analysis of Nedelcho Kolev. Ryvok I Tolchok, 73-76. Translated by Yesis, M. (1981). Soviet Sports Review, 16(3), 114-118.

16. Sparto, P.J., M. Parnianpour, T.E. Reinsel, & S. Simon. (1997). The effect of fatigue on multijoint kinematics, coordination, and postural stability during a repetitive lifting test. The Journal of Orthopaedic and Sports Physical Therapy, 25(1), 3-12.

17. Takano, B. (1987). Coaching optimal technique in the snatch and the clean and jerk, Part II. <u>NSCA Journal, 9</u>(6), 52-56.

18. Takano, B. (1988). Coaching optimal technique in the snatch and the clean and jerk, Part III. <u>NSCA Journal, 10</u>(1), 54-59.

19. Zatsiorsky, V.M. (1994). <u>Science and Practice of Strength Training.</u> Champaign, Il: Human Kinetics, 50-51.

Chapter Three
The Jerk

Chapter Outline:

The Jerk
Exercises to be Mastered First
  Military Press
Progressions for the Jerk

Push Jerk
Squat Jerk
Biomechanical Information on the Jerk

Chapter Objectives:

1. Understand the correct way to perform the split jerk
2. Understand the correct ways to perform the exercises that should be mastered before attempting to learn the jerk
3. Understand the correct ways to perform each of the progressions for the jerk and what the differences are between the various exercises

The jerk is part of the clean and jerk exercise in competition. This exercise is performed second, after the snatch. The jerk and the clean are best learned alone before combining them. This chapter is organized into several sections; the first describes how to perform the jerk, the second describes the exercise that should be mastered before beginning the jerk progressions, and the final section describes the progressions to help with learning the split jerk.

Split Jerk

Purpose of the exercise: This is the competition lift. It is done immediately after the classic (or squat) clean.

Starting position:
1. This exercise begins after the bar has been cleaned to the shoulders or after it has been taken from a squat rack.
2. Take a deep breath, hold it, and set your back.
3. Your elbows should be high.
4. Use a clean-width grip on the bar.
5. After getting the bar to the shoulders, you should take the time to get your feet under your hips - this is the most advantageous positioning for the feet in the jerk (7) (see photo 3-1).

Photo 3-1: The starting position of the split jerk.

Photo 3-2: The dip during the split jerk.

Photo 3-3: The drive during the split jerk.

Dip and drive:

1. From the starting position *quickly* squat down into a quarter squat (see photo 3-2).
2. Without pausing at the bottom, drive up powerfully with the legs.

> The faster you can switch from the dip to the drive, the greater the elastic potential created in the muscles and the higher working effect. Pausing while dipping will result in reduced results in the jerk (1, 5).

3. This dip and drive will force the bar off your shoulders (1, 5) (see photo 3-3).

4. The dip and drive is actually the most important part of the lift; most problems with failed jerks can be traced back to the dip and drive (7).

The split:
1. When the bar has reached its point of maximum ascent, split one foot forward and one back.
2. This will cause you to drop down under the bar and catch it at arm's length.
3. In the split the front leg is bent and the rear leg should be slightly bent as well, this helps to preserve an upright trunk. It is very important that the feet move directly forward and backwards. The front foot will be flat on the ground and the ball of the rear foot should be in contact with the ground.
4. Note that the bar must be CAUGHT at arm's length - a lifter is not allowed to press the bar (1, 5)!
5. The split should begin when the bar begins to pass the face (7) (see photo 3-4).

Recovery:
1. From the split position, move the front foot back into the original starting position.
2. Then move the back foot forward.
3. This order is to maintain balance (5).
4. If the wrong foot moves first, the lifter can lose control of the bar.

Photo 3-4: The split during the split jerk.

Photo 3-5: The end position of the split jerk.

End position:
1. You should be standing straight up with the bar overhead.
2. The back is set and the bar is over your hips for balance.
3. Since catching the bar in the split, you should not once have bent the arms - they should have remained locked out since the split. If the arms are bent it is counted as no lift in competition (see photo 3-5).

Things to remember:
1. The dip, drive, and split must take place *fast;* otherwise this exercise will not work.
2. If you do not go deeply enough into the split, you will not be able to catch the bar at arm's length. However, if you go too deeply in the split (also known as overjerking) the weight will drop after reaching its apex, causing an unlocking of the elbows (and disqualification) (13).
3. The bar must be caught with the arms locked out - and the arms must remain locked out until the lift is over!

Common Errors: Some of the more common errors associated with the split jerk are:
1. Being off balance when the bar is overhead
2. Hitting the chin during the lift
3. Looking down during the jerk
4. Failure to catch the bar with the elbows locked
5. Bending the elbows after catching the bar
6. Failure to split the feet far enough
7. Bringing the rear foot forward first during the recovery

These errors are discussed in detail in chapter ten.

One exercise should be mastered before beginning the progressions for the jerk. It is the military press.

Military Press

Purpose of the exercise: This is a conditioning exercise, but it also teaches you to put the bar over your center of gravity.

Starting position:
1. In the military press, the bar starts off on the front of your shoulders.
2. The bar is on the front of the shoulders, the breath is held, the back is set, and the elbows are high (see photo 3-1).

End position:
1. Press the bar up and slightly behind the head.
2. The bar should be placed over the center of gravity (i.e. over the hips). This is the path the bar will follow during the jerk (see photo 3-5).

Things to remember:
1. Remember, simply pressing the bar straight up is not enough in this exercise. The bar must be pressed up and over the head until the bar is over the hips. It will be very difficult to control the bar if you get off balance.
2. Keep your back set throughout.

Once the above two exercises are mastered, you are ready to begin working on the progressions for the jerk. The progressions for the jerk are (2, 5):
    1. Push Jerk
    2. Squat Jerk

Push Jerk

Purpose of the exercise: The push jerk has several purposes. First, it is an excellent conditioning exercise for the upper body. Second, this exercise helps reinforce the idea of moving the bar up and over the center of gravity. Finally, this exercise helps develop the dip and drive which is critical to good jerk technique (1, 13).

Starting position:
1. The starting position is the same as in the military press.
2. The bar is on the front of the shoulders.
3. Take a deep breath, hold it, then set your back.
4. Your feet should be approximately hip-width apart (1, 5) (see photo 3-1).

Dip and drive:
1. From the starting position *quickly* squat down into a quarter squat (see photo 3-2).
2. Without pausing at the bottom, drive up powerfully with the legs. The faster you can switch from the dip to the drive, the greater the elastic potential created in the muscles and the higher working effect. Pausing while dipping will result in reduced results in the jerk (9).
3. This dip and drive will force the bar off the shoulders (1, 5) (see photo 3-3).

End position:
1. Once the drive has taken place the bar will be forced off the shoulders. If the exercise is done correctly, the bar will start to slow its ascent around the level of the face.
2. From here the bar should be pressed up and overhead just like in the military press.
3. Remember to get the bar over your hips (see photo 3-5)!

Things to remember:
1. The back should remain set throughout the exercise. A set back is critical to balancing the bar overhead.
2. During the dip and drive the elbows need to remain high. In other words, when dipping down do not allow the elbows to drop forward. This will make the exercise harder to do because the bar will be over the toes, rather than over the heel-arch of the foot (13).
3. It is important to place the bar over the hips so that you do not end up off balance.
4. During the dip, make sure it occurs by squatting from the hips - not from the knees.

Common Errors: Some of the more common errors associated with the push jerk are:
1. Being off balance when the bar is overhead
2. Hitting the chin during the lift
3. Looking down during the jerk

These errors are discussed in detail in chapter ten.

The Squat Jerk

Purpose of the Exercise: This exercise is designed to help with speed and balance. Some lifters will also use this variation of the jerk in competition.

Starting Position:
1. The starting position for this exercise is the same as in the push jerk.

Dip and Drive:
1. The dip and drive during this exercise is executed the same as in the push jerk.

Squat:
1. This is the phase of the lift where differences appear.
2. As the bar is driven past your face move your feet to the sides (so that they are about shoulder-width apart). When your feet land on the ground, you should rebend your knees and catch the bar in a squat position. The combination of moving your feet and squatting will move you underneath the bar - enabling you to catch it at arm's length.
3. Remember, when you catch the bar your arms must be locked out.

Things to Remember:
1. This is a much more explosive exercise than the push jerk. The rebending of the knees must happen quickly in order to catch the bar overhead with your arms locked out.
2. Remember to keep the bar over your hips, otherwise you will be off-balance.

Common Errors:
1. Not catching the bar with your arms locked out.
2. Not keeping the bar over your hips.

Biomechanical Information on the Jerk

In competition, the jerk happens quickly. Table 3-1 shows how much time different lifters spend in each phase of the jerk in competition.

Athlete	Dip	Drive	Split
Shary	0.5	0.2	0.4
Rigert	0.5	0.18	0.09
Alexeev	0.52	0.24	0.44
Bonk	0.6	0.28	0.48

Table 3-1: Competition values for the jerk in seconds (8,11,12)
Data from references 8, 11, and 12 is reprinted by permission from Sports Training Inc.

As can be seen from the table, most athletes take right around a second to execute the jerk. Bonk, the last athlete, takes approximately 1.3 seconds to execute the jerk and is criticized by the Soviet authors about his jerk technique (8).

In competition, the bar moves faster during the jerk than during the clean. Various authors report the bar's maximum velocity ranging from 1.5 m/sec to 2.18 m/sec (3, 4, 10, 11, 12).

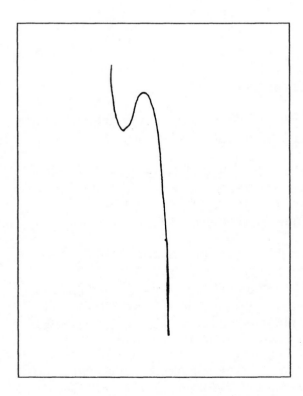

Figure 3-1 Technique of a 175 kg jerk. From Jones, L. (1991). <u>USWF Coaching Accreditation Course Senior Coach Manual</u>, Colorado Spring, CO.: U.S. Weightlifting Federation, 38, reprinted by permission of USA Weightlifting.

Figure 3-1 shows an efficient jerk technique. The lifter performs a vertical dip and drive and keeps the bar over their center of gravity during the dip and drive (6).

36

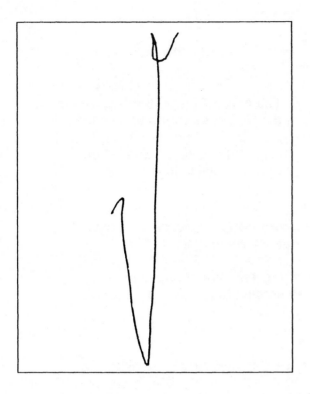

Figure 3-2 Technique of a 125 kg jerk. From Jones, L. (1991). <u>USWF Coaching Accreditation Course Senior Coach Manual</u>, Colorado Spring, CO.: U.S. Weightlifting Federation, 40, reprinted by permission of USA Weightlifting.

Figure 3-2 shows an inefficient jerk. The lifter drops forward during the dip and drive, this causes the bar to be caught forward - so the lifter must step forward to save the lift (6).

References

1. Baker, G. (1987). <u>The United States Weightlifting Federation Coaching Manual Volume I Technique.</u> Colorado Springs, CO.: U.S. Weightlifting Federation, 71-75.
2. Cioroslan, D. (1995). Ask the national coach. <u>Weightlifting U.S.A., 13</u>(2), 5.
3. Garhammer, J. (1981). Biomechanical characteristics of the 1978 world weight-lifting champions. In <u>Biomechanics VIIB: Proceedings of the Seventh International Congress of Biomechanics, Warsaw, Poland.</u> Baltimore, MD: University Park Press, 300-304.
4. Garhammer, J. (1985). Biomechanical profiles of Olympic weightlifters. <u>International Journal of Sport Biomechanics, 1.</u> 122-130.
5. Jones, L. (1991). <u>USWF Coaching Accreditation Course Club Coach Manual.</u> Colorado Springs, CO.: U.S. Weightlifting Federation, 43-44,58-62.
6. Jones, L. (1991). <u>USWF Coaching Accreditation Course Senior Coach Manual</u>, Colorado Spring, CO.: U.S. Weightlifting Federation, , 38, 40.
7. Jones, L. (1995). Coaching platform. <u>Weightlifting U.S.A., 13</u>(5), 6-7.
8. Medvedev, A.S., and Lukashov, A.A. (1977). Jerk technique analysis of world recordholders Alexeev and Bonk. <u>Tyazhelaya Atletika, 1</u>, 60-62. Translated by Yesis, M. (1981). <u>Soviet Sports Review, 16</u>(1), 11-17.
9. Medvedyev, A.S. (1986). <u>A System of Multi-Year Training in Weightlifting.</u> Moscow: Fizkultura i Sport. Translated by Charniga, Jr., A. (1989). Livonia, Michigan: Sportivny Press, 79.

10. Roman, R.A., and Shakirzuanov, M.S. Jerk technique analysis of Nedelcho Kolev. Ryvok I Tolchok, 73-76. Translated by Yesis, M. (1981). Soviet Sports Review, 16(3), 114-118.
11. Roman, R.A., and Shakirzyanov, M.S. (1978). Jerk technique analysis: David Rigert. Ryvok I Tolchok, 1978. Translated by Yesis, M. (1980). Soviet Sports Review,15(3), 127-132.
12. Roman, R.A., and Shakirzyanov, M.S. (1979). Clean and jerk technique of Valery Shary. Tyazhelaya Atletika, 17-21. Translated by Yesis, M. (1980). Soviet Sports Review,15(1), 22-28.
13. Takano, B. (1988). Coaching optimal technique in the snatch and the clean and jerk, Part III. NSCA Journal,10(1), 54-59.

Chapter Four
The Snatch

Chapter Outline:

The Classic (or Squat) Snatch
Determining Grip Width for the Snatch
Learning the Snatch
  Progression #1
    Exercises to be Mastered First
      Behind the Neck Press with a Snatch
      Grip
    Progressions for the Power Snatch
      Hang Snatch from Above the Knees
      Hang Snatch from Below the Knees
      Power Snatch

Progressions for Squatting with the
Barbell Overhead
    Overhead Squat
    Snatch Balance
Progression #2
  Snatch Grip Deadlift
  Snatch Grip Deadlift + Shrug
  Snatch Grip Deadlift + Jump
  Power Snatch
  Overhead Squat
  Power Snatch + Overhead Squat
Biomechanical Information on the
Snatch

Chapter Objectives:

1. Understand the correct way to perform the competition movement
2. Understand the correct ways to perform the exercise that should be mastered before attempting to learn the snatch
3. Understand how and why to perform each of the progressions for the snatch and what the differences are between the various exercises

The snatch is the first lift performed in competition. It is also the most complicated of the two lifts; one reason for this is because in the snatch the velocity of muscle contraction is faster than the clean and jerk (8). Another reason is that in the snatch the acceleration phase is faster than in the clean (6). In other words, things happen in less time during the snatch!

This chapter is organized around several sections; first the classic (a.k.a. squat) snatch will be described; second, you will learn how to determine proper grip width for the snatch; third, two different progressions (like with the clean) will be discussed for learning the snatch - with each of the exercises described. Like with the clean, each has its own benefits and drawbacks.

Squat (or Classic) Snatch

Purpose of the exercise: This is the first lift performed in competition.

Photo 4-1: Starting position of the snatch.

Photo 4-2: The first pull of the snatch.

Starting position:
1. The bar is on the floor.
2. The feet should be hip-width apart.
3. Grip the bar with a snatch-width grip and pull the bar against your shins (see below about how to determine grip width for the snatch).
4. Take a deep breath, hold it, and set your back.
5. Your shoulders should be ahead of the bar, with your chest and abdomen protruding forward (15).
6. Your hips should be higher than your knees in this position and your elbows should be rotated out (see photo 4-1).

First pull:
1. The first pull should be achieved by knee extension. During the first pull your hips and shoulders should rise up at the same speed.
2. Extend your knees until the bar is at knee height.
3. The first pull in this exercise needs to be slow and controlled. If the first pull is too fast it will lead to a decrease in velocity later on - making the lift more difficult (2, 14) (see photo4-2).
4. The arms need to stay straight during the first and second pulls.
5. Remember to keep your back set during the first pull.

Second pull:
1. From knee height, the knees are extended until the bar scrapes the hips (see photo 4-3).
2. Violently extend the hips and elevate the shoulder girdle to explode upward.
3. This explosion is imparting momentum to the bar, making it rise up your body (see photo 4-4).

Photo 4-3: Scraping the hips during the snatch.

Photo 4-4: The second pull of the snatch.

Nonsupport phase:
1. The second pull is followed through by jumping straight up in the air.
2. The momentum generated by the second pull and the jump will force the barbell up along your body and eventually overhead.

Photo 4-5: Amortization phase of the snatch.

Amortization phase:
1. As the bar moves up your body, you should be preparing to move under it and catch it at arm's length in a deep squat.
2. Land with your feet slightly-wider than hip-width apart.
3. Land in a deep squat and catch the barbell overhead - with your arms locked. If this is done right, you should be in a squat position with the knees protruding ahead of the ankles.
4. Your trunk should be upright or slightly inclined forward (15).
5. Remember that your arms must remain locked throughout (see photo 4-5)!

End position:
1. From the squat, stand up - keeping your arms locked.
2. When standing, the chest should be inflated and the back should be set.
3. The arms are still locked out and the bar should be over the hips (see photo 4-6).

Photo 4-6: End position of the snatch.

Things to remember:
1. Speed is critical here.
2. Remember to keep the bar over your hips when it is overhead - otherwise you will lose control of the bar.
3. Keep your back set throughout this movement.

Common Errors: Some of the more common errors associated with the classic snatch are:
1. Failure to "land" on flat feet
2. Failure to catch the bar with locked out arms
3. Bending the elbows after catching the bar
4. Throwing the bar away from the body during the pulls
5. Losing control of the bar after catching it
6. Hitting the knees instead of scraping the hips

7. Bending the elbows during the first and second pulls

These errors are discussed in detail in chapter eleven.

Determining Grip Width for the Snatch

There are two methods for determining grip width for the snatch. With the first method, hold your upper arms horizontal, then have someone measure the distance from elbow to elbow. This distance is then marked on the bar. Then grasp the bar so that the marks lie between your first and second fingers (10) (see photo 4-7).

Photo 4-7: Determining grip width for the snatch, part one.

The second method involves extending one arm directly to the side with your hand making a fist. The distance from the opposite shoulder to the edge of the fist is measured. This distance is then marked on the bar. Then grip the bar outside those marks (10) (see photo 4-8).

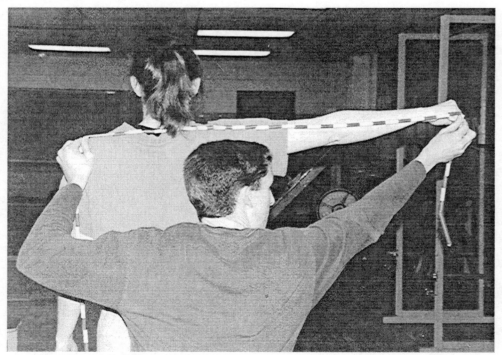

Photo 4-8: Determining grip width for the snatch, part two.

Both methods work equally well, it just depends on what kind of equipment one has around at the time. Also, realize that these measurements are not set in stone - they are starting points. Individuals will vary their grips as they learn the exercises.

Progression #1 for learning the Classic (or Squat) Snatch

One exercise should be mastered before learning the snatch. That exercise is the behind the neck press with a snatch grip. This is because many new lifters do not have the shoulder strength to allow them to squat with a weight overhead; in addition this lift will help teach balance.

Behind the Neck Press with Snatch Grip

Purpose of the exercise: This exercise is for strengthening the shoulders and arms. It also helps to teach balance.

Photo 4-9: Starting position for the behind the neck press, snatch grip.

Starting position:
1. The bar is resting on the back of your shoulders.
2. Grip the bar with a snatch-width grip.
3. Step back from the racks with the bar on the shoulders.
4. Take a deep breath, hold it, then set your back (10) (see photo 4-9).

Photo 4-10: End position of the behind the neck press, snatch grip.

End position:
1. With the bar on the back of the shoulders, press the weight overhead.
2. The bar needs to remain over your hips, to stay over the center of gravity (10) (see photo 4-10).

Things to remember:
1. Because the grip is much wider, not as much weight can be handled as in a jerk grip press.
2. It is important to keep your back set during the lift as this will aid in balance at the top.
3. Remember to keep the bar over your hips while it is overhead.

The progressions for the snatch take two paths. One path prepares you for learning the power snatch while the second path teaches squatting with the barbell overhead. Lifts in the first path include:
1. Hang power snatch from above the knees
2. Hang power snatch from below the knees
3. Power snatch

The lifts in the second path include:
1. Overhead squat
2. Snatch balance
3. The squat snatch

Hang Power Snatch from Above the Knees

Purpose of the exercise: This exercise teaches you to explode with the bar and catch it overhead with the arms fully extended.

Starting position:
1. Grip the bar with a snatch-width grip.
2. Feet are hip-width apart.
3. Stand up with the bar in your hands.
4. Take a deep breath, hold it, and set your back.
5. Bend forward from the hips until the bar is touching your hips (1, 10) (see photo 4-11).

Photo 4-11: Starting position of the hang power snatch from above the knees.

Explosion:
1. Extend your hips and jump straight up into the air while shrugging the shoulders up.
2. You should exert so much force on the bar that it continues to rise up as your body is dropping back down (1, 10). Remember to jump straight up.
3. When landing, your feet should still only be hip-width apart. Avoid splitting your feet to the side; avoid jumping forward or backwards.
4. Your arms should be straight while jumping (see photo 4-4).

End position:
1. The bar will be caught overhead, in a partial squat (see photo 4-12).
2. When the bar is caught overhead your arms should be locked out - the bar cannot be caught on bent arms!
3. From this position, stand straight up.
4. The bar will be overhead, arms locked, back set (see photo 4-5).

Photo 4-12: Catching the bar during the hang power snatch from above the knees.

Things to remember:
1. Your back must be set throughout this exercise otherwise it will be difficult to control the weight overhead.
2. The bar must be kept over your hips during this exercise, otherwise you will lose control of the bar.
3. Speed is essential in this exercise.
4. Remember that the bar must be caught overhead with the arms locked out   otherwise it is no lift!

Common Errors: Some of the more common errors associated with the hang power snatch from above the knees are:
1. The lifter "squats" into position instead of bending forward
2. Splitting the feet to the side during hang or power snatches
3. Failure to "land" on flat feet
4. Failure to catch the bar with locked out arms
5. Bending the elbows after catching the bar
6. Throwing the bar away from the body
7. Losing control of the bar after catching it

These errors are discussed in detail in chapter eleven.

Hang Power Snatch from Below the Knees

Purpose of the exercise: This exercise helps teach how to move the bar around the knees, as well as reinforcing the idea of keeping the bar close to the body (1, 10).

Starting position:
1. Grab the bar and stand up.
2. Take a deep breath and set your back.
3. Bend forward from the hips until the bar is at hip level.
4. Bend the knees until the bar is resting at a level that is below the knees (1, 10) (see photo 4-13).

Photo 4-13: Starting position of the hang power snatch from below the knees.

Explosion:
1. This exercise begins by extending the knees.
2. Once the bar has reached hip level, the bar should scrape the hips and you should jump straight up as in the previous exercise (see photo 4-3).
3. Remember to catch the bar overhead with the arms locked out (10)!

End position:
1. The end position is the same as in the previous exercises.

Things to remember:
1. Use knee extension to get the bar from below the knees to hip level, then use the hips and shoulder girdle to get the bar from hip level to overhead.
2. Speed is critical in this exercise.
3. Remember to catch the bar overhead with the arms locked out!

Common Errors: Some of the more common errors associated with the hang power snatch from above the knees are:
1. The lifter "squats" into position instead of bending forward
2. Splitting the feet to the side during hang or power snatches
3. Failure to "land" on flat feet
4. Failure to catch the bar with locked out arms
5. Bending the elbows after catching the bar
6. Throwing the bar away from the body
7. Losing control of the bar after catching it
8. Hitting the knees instead of scraping the thigh

These errors are discussed in detail in chapter eleven.

Power Snatch

Purpose of the exercise: In addition to teaching how to lift the bar off the floor, this exercise is also used in weightlifting and in athletics as a strength and power builder (10).

Starting position:
1. The bar is on the floor.
2. Grip the bar with a snatch-width grip.
3. Your feet should be hip-width apart.
4. Pull the bar against the shins.
5. Your hips should be higher than your knees in this position.
6. Take a deep breath, hold it, and set your back (10).
7. Your shoulders should be ahead of the bar with your chest and abdomen protruding forward (15).
8. The elbows should be rotated out (see photo 4-1) (13).

First pull:
1. The first pull is still achieved by knee extension.
2. Extend the knees until the bar is at knee height.
3. The first pull in this exercises needs to be slow and controlled. If the first pull is too fast it will lead to a decrease in velocity later on - making the lift more difficult (2, 14) (see photo 4-2).

Second pull:
1. From knee height, the knees are extended until the bar scrapes the hips.
2. Use the hips and shoulder girdle to explode upward.
3. This explosion is imparting momentum to the bar, making it rise up the body (see photos 4-3 and 4-4).

Nonsupport phase:
1. Follow through with the second pull by jumping straight up off the ground.
2. The bar is still traveling up during this phase.
3. Remember, land with the feet roughly hip-width apart.

Amortization phase:
1. Catch the bar with the arms locked out overhead.
2. You should be in a partial squat with your feet hip-width apart.
3. Your back should be set (see photo 4-12).

End position:
1. From the receiving position, stand up, keeping the arms locked out (see photo 4-6).

Things to remember:
1. The first pull should be slow and controlled, the second pull should be explosive.
2. Keep your back set throughout and remember to keep your arms locked out once the bar is caught overhead!

Common Errors: Some of the more common errors associated with the power snatch are:
1. Splitting the feet to the side during hang or power snatches
2. Failure to "land" on flat feet
3. Failure to catch the bar with locked out arms
4. Bending the elbows after catching the bar
5. Throwing the bar away from the body
6. Losing control of the bar after catching it
7. Hitting the knees instead of scraping the thigh
8. Bending the elbows during the first and second pulls

These errors are discussed in detail in chapter eleven.

Overhead Squat

Purpose of the exercise: This exercise serves a number of functions. It teaches you to balance the bar when squating with the weight overhead. It teaches the bottom position of the classic snatch. It also conditions the muscles that must hold the weight overhead. This is an excellent conditioning exercise - but it is often a hard one to learn.

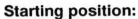

Photo 4-14: Starting position of the overhead squat.

Starting position:
1. Start with the bar on the back of your shoulders.
2. Grip the bar with a snatch-width grip.
3. Step back from the squat rack.
4. Press the weight overhead and lock out your elbows.
5. Take a deep breath, hold it, and set your back.
6. Your feet should be wider than hip-width apart (i.e. squat stance) (10) (see photo 4-14).

The squat:
1. With your arms locked out, squat down as far as is comfortable.
2. Remember to keep your back set and your chest inflated.
3. Push against the bar as you are squatting down (1, 10) (see photo 4-15).

Photo 4-15: Bottom position of the overhead squat.

End position:
1. Upon reaching the low position, reverse direction until you are standing up once again with the bar overhead.

Things to remember:
1. For this exercise to work, a number of things have to happen:
2. Your chest must be inflated and your back must be set.
3. Your feet must stay flat on the floor.
4. Your arms need to stay locked out throughout the exercise.
5. Finally, the bar needs to stay over your hips throughout.
6. If these things don't happen, you will lose control of the bar.

Snatch Balance

Purpose of the exercise: This exercise teaches dropping under the bar and adds a speed component to the overhead squat. It also helps to develop the footwork for the squat snatch (1).

Starting position:
1. Start with the bar on the back of your shoulders.
2. The grip on the bar should be snatch-width.
3. Your feet should only be hip-width apart (also known as pulling position).
4. From this position, take a deep breath, hold it, and set your back (1, 10) (see photo 4-16).

Photo 4-16: Starting position of the snatch balance.

Photo 4-17: Dip during the snatch balance.

Dip and drive:

1. From the start position, quickly dip down with your legs and then drive the weight off your shoulders (see photos 4-17 and 4-18).
2. As the weight is driven off your shoulders, quickly jump your feet into squat position (i.e. wider than hip-width apart) and drop under the bar - catching it in the full squat, with your arms locked (1, 10) (see photo 4-16).

Photo 4-18: Drive during the snatch balance.

End position:
1. You should be in a full squat, with your feet wider than hip-width apart.
2. The bar will be overhead with your arms locked out.
3. Your chest should be elevated with your back set.
4. From here, stand up with the bar overhead.

Things to remember:
1. When the bar is driven off your shoulders drop down into the squat very quickly.
2. Remember to keep the bar over your hips.
3. When dropping into the squat, use your arms to push yourself down (1).

Progression #2 for learning the snatch

Like the first progression, this one involves exercises that should be mastered first before moving on to the other exercises. The exercises that should be mastered first is the snatch grip deadlift.

Deadlift, Snatch Grip

Purpose of the Exercise: Essentially, this exercise teaches the first pull of the snatch. It is also useful in conditioning the muscles of the lower body and back that are responsible for moving the bar during the first pull.

Starting Position:
1. The bar is on the floor.
2. The feet are approximately hip-width apart.
3. Have the bar resting against your shins.
4. Squat down, putting your stomach between the legs.
5. Grip the bar with a snatch-width grip.
6. Take a deep breath, hold it, then set your back.
7. Your shoulders should be slightly in front of the bar and your elbows should be rotated out. Your chest and abdomen should be protruding.
8. Your hips should be higher than your knees in this position (see photo 4-1).

Ending Position:
1. From the starting position extend your legs so that the bar is raised off the ground.
2. Continue to drive with your legs until the bar touches your leg at hip level (see photo 4-3).
3. Make sure to keep your back set as your pick the bar up.
4. Note that your shoulders and hips should travel up at the same speed.

Things to Remember:
1. This should be a slow and controlled exercise. Technique is extremely important on this exercise.

Common Errors:
1. Having the hips travel up faster than the shoulders - This is an inefficient way to lift the bar and results in more strain on the lower back.
2. Loss of back set while lifting.

Once those exercises have been mastered you are ready to move on to the progressions for learning the snatch. Those exercises are:
1. Deadlift, snatch grip + Shrug
2. Deadlift, snatch grip + Jump
3. Power Snatch
4. Overhead Squat
5. Power Snatch + Overhead Squat

Deadlift, snatch grip + Shrug

Purpose of the Exercise: This is not a conditioning exercise; it is merely presented to help teach the movement patterns associated with learning the clean. After it has been mastered it should be discontinued.

Starting Position:
1. This exercise has the same starting position as the deadlift.

Deadlift:
1. This part of the exercise is performed just like during the deadlift.

Shrug:
1. Once the bar has reached hip level extend your hips.
   As your hips extend, rise up on your toes and shrug your shoulders up.
2. Rising on your toes and shrugging should happen at the same time.

Things to Remember:
1. Make sure that when you rise up on your toes and shrug that these activities happen at the same time.

Deadlift, snatch grip + Jump

Purpose of the Exercise: This is not a conditioning exercise, it is merely presented to help teach the movement patterns associated with learning the snatch. After it has been mastered it should be discontinued. This exercise is designed to help teach technique for the first and second pulls.

Starting Position:
1. The starting position is the same as in the deadlift.

Deadlift:
1. Lift the bar until it reaches hip level, just like in the deadlift.

Jump:
1. Once the bar has reached hip level jump straight up into the air and shrug your shoulders up.
2. The jump and shrug should happen at the same time (see photo 4-4).

Ending Position:
1. Make sure, when landing, that your feet land in the same place they started from.

Power Snatch + Overhead Squat

This is a combination exercise and is an excellent conditioning exercise as well as a teaching tool. In this exercise the lifter performs a specified number of power snatches. After the last snatch has been performed, while the bar is still overhead, the lifter will perform a number of overhead squats. This is a very strenuous exercise and is good for reinforcing the importance of keeping the back set, the elbows locked out, balance, and keeping the bar over the hips.

Comments on the Different Progressions

Both progressions have their strong and weak points. The first progression involves a systematic learning process of all the components of the snatch. It probably leads to a more thorough understanding of technique and position. However, the first progression also takes longer to work your way through - some lifters may take months to work through all the progressions.

The second progression has the benefit of speed - lifters can move through it in a matter of days. The principal drawback to this progression is that lifters then to learn to perform the lift in parts: i.e. they learn to pull the bar to their hips, then they learn to snatch the bar from that hip-level position. This is a difficult habit to break them of, and it is also illegal in competition. Coaches and lifters must continually stress the need to blend the parts together when learning the second progression.

Biomechanical Information on the Snatch

Similar to the clean, in the snatch the second pull should take less time than the first pull (3, 5, 12). As in the clean, the bar will also attain a greater velocity during the second pull when compared with the first pull (3, 9).

During the snatch, the bar should move faster than in the clean or in the jerk. Garhammer and Lee, et al. have reported that in international competition, men are moving the bar at between 1.79-2.29 m/sec when performing the snatch (4, 5, 6, 12). Compare this with the values for the clean and the jerk. Garhammer and Lee, et al. also report that women lifters are able to move the bar at speeds of between 1.94-2.28 m/sec (6, 7, 12).

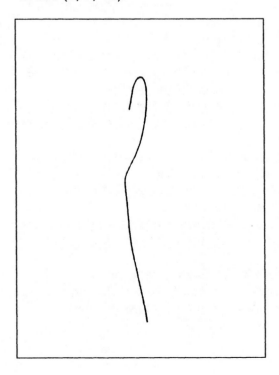

Figures 4-1 shows an efficient snatch technique. The bar moves towards the lifter until the second pull and the drop under the bar phases, when it begins to swing away some (11).

Figure 4-1 Technique of a 160 kg snatch. From Jones, L. (1991). USWF Coaching Accreditation Course Senior Coach Manual, Colorado Spring, CO.: U.S. Weightlifting Federation, 36, reprinted by permission of USA Weightlifting.

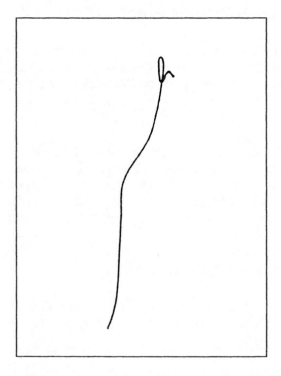

Figures 4-2 shows an inefficient snatch technique. Figure **4-2** shows the lifter swinging the bar away from the body during the first and second pulls, resulting in a forward jump to catch the bar (11).

Figure 4-2 Technique of a 140 kg snatch. From Jones, L. (1991). <u>USWF Coaching Accreditation Course Senior Coach Manual</u>, Colorado Spring, CO.: U.S. Weightlifting Federation, 38, reprinted by permission of USA Weightlifting.

References

1. Baker, G. (1987). <u>The United States Weightlifting Federation Coaching Manual Volume I Technique.</u> Colorado Springs, CO.: U.S. Weightlifting Federation, 41-55.
2. Bartonietz, K.E. (1996). Biomechanics of the snatch: Toward a higher training efficiency. <u>Strength and Conditioning, 18</u>(3), 24-31.
3. Frolov, V.I., Lelikov, S.I., Efimov, N.M., and Vanagas, M.P. (1977). Snatch technique of top-class weightlifters. <u>Teoriya I Praktika Fizicheskoi Kultury,6</u>, 59-61. Translated by Yesis, M. (1979). <u>Soviet Sports Review, 14</u>(1), 24-29.
4. Garhammer, J. (1981). Biomechanical characteristics of the 1978 world weightlifting champions. In <u>Biomechanics VIIB: Proceedings of the Seventh International Congress of Biomechanics, Warsaw, Poland.</u> Baltimore: University Park Press, 300-304.
5. Garhammer, J. (1985). Biomechanical profiles of Olympic weightlifters. <u>International Journal of Sport Biomechanics, 1</u>, 122-130.
6. Garhammer, J. (1990). Bar trajectories of world champion male and female weightlifters. <u>International Olympic Lifter, 10</u>(6), 12-13.
7. Garhammer, J. (1991). A comparison of maximal power outputs between elite male and female weightlifters in competition. <u>International Journal of Sport Biomechanics, 7</u>, 3-11.
8. Hakkinen, K., P.V. Komi, & H. Kauhanen. (1986). Electromyographic and force production characteristics of leg extensor muscles of elite weight lifters during isometric, concentric, and various stretch-shortening cycle exercises. <u>International Journal of Sports Medicine, 7</u>, 144-151.

9. Isaka, T., J. Okado, & K. Funato. (1996). Kinematic analysis of the barbell during the snatch movement of elite Asian weight lifters. <u>Journal of Applied Biomechanics, 12</u>, 508-516.

10. Jones, L. (1991). <u>USWF Coaching Accreditation Course Club Coach Manual.</u> Colorado Springs, CO.: U.S. Weightlifting Federation, 44-46, 50-57, 62.

11. Jones, L. (1991). <u>USWF Coaching Accreditation Course Senior Coach Manual</u>, Colorado Spring, CO.: U.S. Weightlifting Federation, 36, 38

12. Lee, Y.-H., Huwang, C-Y., Tsuang, Y-H. (1995). Biomechanical characteristics of preactivation and pulling phases of snatch lift. <u>Journal of Applied Biomechanics,11</u>, 288-298.

13. Medvedev, A.S. (1989). Three periods of the snatch and clean and jerk. <u>NSCA Journal,10</u>(6), 33-38.

14. Medvedyev, A.S. (1986). <u>A System of Multi-Year Training in Weightlifting.</u> Moscow: Fizkultura I Sport. Translated by Charniga, Jr., A. (1989). Livonia, Michigan: Sportivny Press,. 53-59, 77.

15. Takano, B. (1987). Coaching optimal technique in the snatch and clean and jerk, Part I. <u>NSCA Journal, 9</u>(5), 50-59.

Chapter Five
Assistance Exercises

Chapter Outline:

Squats
Bend Overs
  Hyperextensions
  Good Mornings
   Standing
   Seated
   Floor

Pulls
Clean Assistance Exercises
Jerk Assistance Exercises
Snatch Assistance Exercises
Olympic Lifting and the Bench Press

Chapter Objectives:

1. Understand the various classes of assistance exercises for Olympic lifting
2. Understand the correct ways to perform the various assistance exercises
3. Understand why the various assistance exercises are used in training

Assistance exercises are important because they help to strengthen the soft tissue of the joints (6). They also help to reinforce good technique. Generally, assistance exercises fall into one of several categories:

    1. Squats
    2. Bend Overs
    3. Pulls
    4. Clean assistance exercises
    5. Jerk assistance exercises
    6. Snatch assistance exercises

Back and Front Squats

Squats are used to develop strength, speed, and also to help perfect technique (4,7). They should be included in every workout. Generally, weightlifters do squats in the 70-85% of max range.

Bend Overs

Bend overs are a group of lower-back strengthening exercises (7). This family of exercises include things like hyperextensions, good mornings, and Romanian deadlifts.

Good Mornings

Good mornings are designed to strengthen the muscles of the lower back. These exercises also work the hamstrings and gluteal muscles. There are three types of good mornings that this book covers:
1. Good Mornings, Standing
2. Good Mornings, Seated
3. Good Mornings from the Floor

Photo 5-1: Starting position of the good morning.

Good Mornings, Standing

Starting position:
1. Place the bar on the back of your shoulders.
2. Step away from the squat rack, take a deep breath, and set your back.
3. Make sure your feet are approximately hip-width apart (see photo 5-1).

End position:
1. From the starting position, bend forward *from the hips*.
2. While the knees should be slightly bent throughout the exercise all the movement should come from the hips.
3. Once you have reached the lowest position, extend your hips until you are standing straight up again (see photo 5-2).

Photo 5-2: Ending position of the good morning.

Things to remember:
1. This exercise is an excellent strengthener for the lower-back muscles.
2. However, it can be highly dangerous if done incorrectly or with too much weight.
3. Beginners should progress very slowly and cautiously on this exercise.

Common Errors: Some common errors associated with good mornings are:
1. Failure to keep the back set
2. Bending the knees excessively

Photo 5-3: Starting position of the seated good morning.

Photo 5-4: Ending position of the seated good morning.

Good Mornings, Seated

Starting position:
1. Sit down on a bench and place the bar on the back of your shoulders.
2. Set your back (see photo 5-3).

End position:
1. From the starting position, bend forward *from the hips.*
2. The idea is to touch the bench with your chest and face (see photo 5-4).
3. Once you have reached the lowest position, extend the hips until you are sitting straight up again.

Things to remember:
1. This exercise is an excellent strengthener for the lower-back muscles.
2. However, it can be highly dangerous if done incorrectly or with too much weight.
3. Beginners should progress very slowly and cautiously on this exercise.
4. Flexibility is a much bigger factor in this variation of the good morning and will limit how far down you can go.
5. It is critical that you keep your back set throughout the exercise.

Common Errors: Some common errors associated with good mornings are:
1. Failure to keep the back set

Good Mornings from the Floor

Starting position:
1. The bar is on the floor.
2. Grip the bar with either a clean-width or a snatch-width grip.
3. Pull the bar against your shins.
4. Set your back. Your hips should be higher than your knees on this exercise - in fact your hips/shoulders/back should be parallel to the floor at the start - this is an exaggerated starting position (see photo 5-5).

End position:
1. From the starting position extend your hips, keeping your knees bent, until you are standing straight up. The bar should touch either your hips (snatch-grip) or your thighs (clean-grip).
2. Remember, all the motion for this exercise comes from rotation about your hip joint - your knees do not move at all.
3. Remember to keep you back set (see photo 5-6).

Photo 5-5: Starting position of the good morning from the floor.

Photo 5-6: Ending position of the good morning from the floor.

Things to remember:
1. This exercise is an excellent strengthener for the lower-back muscles.
2. However, it can be highly dangerous if done incorrectly or with too much weight.

3. Beginners should progress very slowly and cautiously on this exercise.
4. It is critical that you keep your back set throughout the exercise.
5. Many lifters will try to deadlift the bar on this exercise, instead of letting the movement come from rotation about the hip joint. Your knees should not move during this exercise.

Common Errors: Some common errors associated with good mornings are:
1. Failure to keep the back set
2. Using your knees to lift the barbell.

Romanian Deadlifts
Romanian deadlifts are another low back/hamstring/glute developer.

Starting Position:
1. Take a clean-width or snatch-width grip on the barbell.
2. Stand up with the barbell in your hands.
3. Set your back (see photo 5-7).

Ending Position:
1. Bend forward from your hips.
2. The barbell should slide along your legs as you bend forward - i.e. do not let the bar get away from your body.
3. Once the bar gets to a point just below your knees, stop. Hold this position for a count (see photo 5-8).
4. Reverse the direction by extending your hips until you are standing up once again.

Photo 5-7: Starting position of the Romanian deadlift.

Photo 5-8: Ending position of the Romanian deadlift.

Things to Remember:
1. Remember to keep your back set throughout.
2. The bar needs to be kept close to your body during this exercise.

Common Errors:
1. Not keeping the back set during this exercise.
2. Letting the bar get away from the body.
3. Performing the movements by knee bend instead of hip flexion.

Pulls

Pulls are kinetically and kinematically very similar to the lifts they assist (6). Basically, pulls combine the first and second pulls of the movement but the lifter remains in contact with the floor throughout. These exercises are designed to perfect the technique of the first and second pulls and to develop speed-strength in the athlete. Some authors recommend that they only be performed after a lifter has been training for 1-3 years. Prior to that time power snatches and power cleans will be more effective in training technique and speed-strength (7). Pulls are done with either a snatch-width grip or with a clean-width grip. In an experienced lifter's workout, they are done daily (7).

A pull from the floor may be executed with up to 10% or more above an athlete's maximum competition weight in the clean or snatch (3,6). However, when the weight reaches 100% or more of competition values, technique will break down and the pull will not resemble the lift it is meant to train (3,6). With a load on the bar equal to or greater than maximum competition weight, the bar will be pulled to a lower height, reach a lesser maximum vertical velocity, resulting in a smaller peak propulsion force, and resulting in lower mechanical output than the competition lift it is meant to train (3). Pulls are best performed with weights equaling 90-95% of maximum snatches or cleans. At this weight the pulls are still very similar to the lifts they are meant to train (2,7).

The Pull

Purpose of the exercise: To help train technique, speed, and strength in the first and second pulls.

Photo 5-9: Starting position of the pull (clean pulls are shown in these examples).

Starting position:
1. The bar is on the platform.
2. Approach the bar and position your feet approximately hip-width apart.
3. Grip the bar with either a snatch grip (for snatch pulls) or a clean grip (for clean pulls).
4. The bar should be pulled against your shins.
5. Take a deep breath, hold it, and set your back.
6. Your hips should be higher than the knees.

7. Your elbows should be locked out and rotated to the sides (see photo 5-9).

Photo 5-10: The first pull.

First pull:
1. To get the bar to knee height, extend your knees.
2. The first pull is executed in a slow controlled manner (see photo 5-10).

Second pull:
1. Once the bar is at knee height, continue to extend your knees until the bar scrapes your thigh at mid-thigh level.
2. From here, extend your hips, rise up on your toes, and shrug your shoulders up violently in the same motion.
3. Remember to keep your arms locked out (see photo 5-11)!

End position:
1. Your feet will not leave the platform during the execution of this lift.
2. Once the pull has been executed, the bar goes back on the platform and you should begin again.

Photo 5-11: The second pull.

Things to remember:
1. It is important that the arms stay straight throughout the exercise. Bending the elbows may cause you to develop a habit of doing that - which will slow you down while doing the competition lifts.
2. Remember to keep the bar close to your body during the pull; don't push the bar away.

Common Errors: Some common errors associated with pulls are:
1. Bending the elbows during the pull.
2. Throwing the bar away from the body

Clean assistance exercises

There are several exercises that should be employed extensively in a conditioning program to help develop the clean. Front squats are an excellent conditioning exercise. They not only strengthen the muscles of the lower body, but they also train the lifter to balance heavy weights on the front of the shoulders during a squat.

Photo 5-12: Starting position for cleans from blocks, bar is above the knees.

Clean pulls are good for improving technique and for training speed and strength. Pulls should not be limited to being done form the floor. They can also be done from the hang (above the knees, from the knees, or from below the knees) or from blocks (see photos 5-12 and 5-13). In addition, the deadlift with a clean grip can be used to help strengthen and develop technique on the first pull.

Hang cleans, cleans from blocks, and power cleans are also good conditioners for the clean. When the clean is performed from above the knee level it contributes to improving the speed of the squat-under portion of the lift (amortization phase) (4). The closer the bar is started towards the floor, the more the exercise will develop the first and second pulls (3).

During the power clean the barbell is pulled to a greater height, reaches a greater vertical velocity, and therefore results in greater peak propulsion forces than the squat clean. Therefore, the power clean is a useful exercise in improving speed of movement and power (3). Generally, with training power clean results will be equal to 80-90% of an athlete's maximum squat clean (3, 7).

Photo 5-13: Starting position for cleans from blocks, bar is below the knees.

Jerk assistance exercises

Pressing exercises and triceps exercises are used to help develop the jerk. Pressing exercises strengthen the arms and shoulder girdle - however *pressing exercises do not have a direct effect on results in the snatch and the clean-and-jerk* (7). This needs to be pointed out. The results in the jerk (and indeed in the snatch) depend on speed and strength from the legs, proper coordination, and balance.

Presses can be performed from behind-the-neck and from in front of the neck. Also a good assistance exercise for the jerk is the push jerk. Once again, the push jerk does not contribute to speed but it will train strength (6).

Snatch assistance exercises

There are several exercises that should be employed extensively in a conditioning program to help develop the snatch. Back squats are an excellent conditioning exercise. They not only strengthen the muscles of the lower body, but they also train the lifter to balance heavy weights over their center of gravity during a squat.

Snatch pulls are good for improving technique and for training speed and strength. Pulls should not be limited to being done form the floor. They can also be done from the hang (above the knees, from the knees, or from below the knees) or from blocks (see photos 5-12 and 5-13). In addition, the deadlift with a snatch grip can be used to help strengthen and develop technique on the first pull.

Hang snatches, snatches from blocks, and power snatches are also good conditioners for the snatch. When the snatch is performed from above the knee level it contributes to improving the speed of the squat-under portion of the lift (amortization phase) (4). The closer the bar is started towards the floor, the more the exercise will develop the first and second pulls (3).

During the power snatch the barbell is pulled to a greater height, reaches a greater vertical velocity, and therefore results in greater peak propulsion forces than the squat snatch. Therefore, the power snatch is a useful exercise in improving speed of movement and power (3). Generally, with training power snatch results will be equal to 80-90% of an athlete's maximum squat snatch (3, 7).

Overhead squats and snatch balances should also be included in a program. While neither of these exercises imitates the squat snatch exactly, both help develop certain parts of the movement. The overhead squat gets lifters comfortable with the bottom position of the snatch and also strengthens those muscles that must support weight overhead in a squat. The snatch balance requires perfect technique to hit the bottom position quickly.

A word about bench presses and olympic lifting: The bench press is a great conditioning exercise for the muscles of the chest, shoulders, and triceps. However, excessive bench pressing can be detrimental to olympic lifting. Bench pressing tends to reduce the mobility of the sterno-clavicular joint. This means it becomes more difficult to "rack" the bar when doing the clean, jerk, or front squat. Care must be taken that flexibility is preserved at that joint if one is doing a large amount of bench pressing (5).

References

1. Baker, G (ed.). (1987). The United States Weightlifting Federation Coaching Manual Volume I Technique. Colorado Springs, CO.: U.S. Weightlifting Federation, 32-33.
2. Frolov, V.I., & A.A. Lukashev. (1978). A comparative analysis of snatch and clean technique. Tyazhelaya Atletika, 26-28. Translated by Yesis, M. (1979). Soviet Sports Review, 14(2), 80-82.
3. Garhammer, J., & B. Takano. (1992). Training for weightlifting. In Komi, P.V.(ed.) Strength and Power in Sport (pp. 357-369). International Olympic Committee.
4. Jones, L. (1991). USWF Coaching Accreditation Course Club Coach Manual. Colorado Springs, CO.: U.S. Weightlifting Federation, 43-61.
5. Jones, L. (1991). USWF Coaching Accreditation Course Senior Coach Manual. Colorado Springs, CO.: U.S. Weightlifting Federation, 106.
6. Medvedyev, A.S. (1986). A System of Multi-Year Training in Weightlifting. Moscow: Fizkultura i Sport. Translated by Charniga, Jr., A. (1989). Livonia, Michigan: Sportivny Press, 42, 66, 68, 71.
7. Roman, R.A. (1986). The Training of the Weightlifter. Moscow: Fizkultura i Spovt. Translated by Charniga, Jr., A., Livonia, Michigan: Sportivny Press, 51, 61-71, 103.

PART TWO: PROGRAM DESIGN AND PERIODIZATION

This section is designed to introduce the reader to what goes into designing a year-long periodized training program for weightlifters. There are three chapters in this part of the book: chapter six provides basic background information to the concepts that are used in the following chapters, chapter seven takes the reader through how to design a workout plan for an absolute beginner, chapter eight builds upon the ideas expressed in the proceeding chapters and applies them to intermediate level lifters.

Chapters seven and eight are difficult to write references for because I have pulled ideas from a multitude of sources and adapted them. As a result I have presented an annotated reference page at the end of these chapters. Where I pulled direct ideas from a source, that source is cited in the text.

There are a number of approaches to designing a training program for lifters, different schools of thought as it were. I have drawn the workout programs in chapters seven and eight from three different schools - I've taken what I like about each. From the Soviet model as explained in Medvedyev's books I have employed their organizational structure for training cycles and their emphasis on the need for systematic planning. In addition, early in the training cycles I use their variety of exercises. From Mike Stone's periodization model I have employed the systematic increasing in intensity as the training cycle progresses - I like this approach better than the "random" nature of some of the Eastern European variants. Lastly, as the lifter gets closer to competition their workouts are simplified - so this aspect bears some resemblance to Bulgarian techniques.

Chapters seven and eight are written for a generic (male or female) college-age lifter. This needs to be taken into account when reading them, as these programs are not suitable for everyone!

Chapter Six
General Program Design

Chapter Outline:

Terms
  Volume
  Intensity
Exercise Categories
  Snatch
  Snatch Combination
  Clean and Jerk
  Clean and Jerk Combination
  Pulls
  Squats
  Bend Overs
  Presses
Misc. Program Design Notes
  Exercise Selection
  Exercise Order

Periodization Basics
  What periodization is
  Goals of periodization in weightlifting
  Training blocks
   Macrocycles
   Mesocycles
    General Preparation
    Special Preparation
    Competition
    Transitional
   Microcycles
  Manipulating variables during training blocks
Warming Up and Flexibility

Chapter Objectives:

1. Understand what is meant by volume and intensity.
2. Understand what the various exercise categories are and what exercises are included in each.
3. Be familiar with what periodization is and what its goals are.
4. Understand each of the different training blocks in periodization.
5. Understand what variables are manipulated during periodization.
6. Know how and why to warm up and train flexibility in weightlifting.

This chapter is meant as an introduction to program design in weightlifting. This chapter is broken down into several sections:
1. Terms
2. Exercise Categories
3. Miscellaneous Program Design Notes
4. Periodization Basics
5. Warming Up/ Flexibility

Terms

Program design for weightlifting involves the extensive use of two terms:
1. Volume
2. Intensity

Volume

Volume refers to the amount of work done. Generally in weightlifting it is expressed as the number of lifts (NL) a lifter performs. NL's a workout, week, month, cycle, year, etc. (6)

The more an exercise is repeated, the greater the training stimulus. There is a fine balance that needs to be achieved here, because the number of repetitions should not be so large that the structure of the exercise is disturbed (8). This statement means that if you do too many repetitions per set, with too much weight, you will begin to use bad technique when lifting the weights. You will also begin to perform the movements slowly. This can lead to the building of bad habits that may show up in competition, limiting potential.

Generally you should perform sets of no more than 3-4 repetitions on the speed exercises (i.e. competition movements and their variations) (4, 6). In some cases (with light weights) you can go up to 6 repetitions or more per set. With heavy weights, it is not uncommon for lifters to do sets of 1 and 2 reps per set. In fact this is actually important for the training of weight-lifters. Single-effort work, even with light weights, should be done daily. This helps to develop the ability to concentrate neuro-muscular effort and produces a large effect in terms of absolute strength (9). Weightlifting is a sport concerned with how much weight a person can lift one time; as a result lifters should spend some time developing this skill.

Weightlifters will generally do between 3 and 8 *work out* sets per exercise - i.e. 3 to 8 sets not counting the warm up sets (4, 6). In some cases they may do more. Generally, the fewer the repetitions, the more sets - and vice versa (6).

When starting out, you should be working with 3 sets an exercise (not counting warm up sets). With the speed exercises you should stick to 3-4 reps/set, with the strength exercises (i.e. squats, pulls, bend overs, and presses) up to 5-6 reps/set (4).

One thing to note: If you are unable to complete the prescribed number of repetitions in a set, then you should reduce the number of repetitions - not necessarily the weight (unless it is causing technique to break down) (6).

Intensity

Intensity refers to how difficult the work is. Training effectiveness depends greatly on the weight that is used (16). The most effective intensity range for the development of weightlifting strength is with 65-100% of max (6). Having said that, it should be noted that limit lifts (100% of max) should not be done more than 1-2 sets in a workout and not more often than every 7-10 days (9, 16).

When beginning in a weightlifting program, it is often difficult to judge how much weight to be using. After all, if you are learning the exercises it is difficult to have maximum values of which to determine a percentage. Lyn Jones recommends that on high-skill exercises, the weight should be increased (for beginners) until the technique starts to break down. On the strength exercises, the weight should be the most that you can handle for a specified number of repetitions (i.e. train to failure on the strength exercises) (4).

You should not use so much weight on the speed exercises as to cause muscular failure! When this is allowed to happen there is a good chance that you will get sloppy in you technique and get injured (10).

There are two types of intensity; relative intensity and total intensity:

Relative intensity is expressed as a percentage of the lifter's one repetition maximum (1-RM). In other words, if you can clean 100 kg, then training at 80 kg on one day would mean you are training at a relative intensity of 80%.

Total intensity is the total amount of work done (i.e. sets x reps x weight lifted). It can be expressed in terms of a workout, a week, a month, etc. For example, if you perform a workout with 1 set of 3 reps at 60 kg, 1 set of 3 reps at 80 kg, and 3 sets of 2 reps at 100 kg, then your total intensity for that workout is 1020 kg.

Volume and intensity are both important not only in the planning of training, but in the monitoring of training effectiveness. Their manipulation is one of the foundations of periodization (see chapters 7 and 8 for more about this).

Exercise Categories

To make the planning of training easier, weightlifting exercises are generally broken down into categories. In this book they are broken down into eight categories:

1. Snatch exercises
2. Snatch combination exercises
3. Clean and Jerk exercises
4. Clean and Jerk combination exercises
5. Pulls
6. Squats
7. Bend Overs
8. Presses

Snatch Exercises: This category refers to the classic snatch, power snatch, classic/power snatches from the hang, and classic/power snatches from blocks. In addition, this category also includes the overhead squat and snatch balance.

Snatch Combination Exercises: This category is for exercises combining the snatch (classic or power) with another movement (such as pulls). Examples of some exercises that could be included in this category are: pulls + classic/power snatch (from the floor, hang, or blocks), classic/power snatch (from the floor, hang, or blocks) + overhead squats, or even pulls + snatch + overhead squat.

Clean and Jerk Exercises: This category refers to the classic clean, power clean, classic/power cleans form the hang, classic/power cleans from blocks, split jerk, push jerk, and squat jerk.

Clean and Jerk Combination Exercises: This category is for exercises combining the clean or jerk with other movements. Some examples are: classic/power clean (from the floor, hang, or blocks) + front squats, classic/power clean (from the floor, hang, or blocks) + split/squat/push jerk, front squat + jerk, etc.

Squats: Back and front squats are in this category.

Pulls: Snatch and clean pulls fall into this category. Pulls from the floor, from the hang, and from blocks. For more advanced lifters things like pulls with no explosion, pulls with stops, etc. could be included in this category.

Bend Overs: This category includes hyperextensions, good mornings (standing), good mornings (seated), and good mornings (from the floor).

Presses: This category includes military presses (standing/seated) and behind the neck presses (jerk grip, snatch grip, snatch grip from a squat).

Miscellaneous Program Design Notes

This section discusses two important areas:
1. Exercise selection
2. Exercise order

Exercise Selection

Workouts should emphasize either the snatch or the clean and jerk. If this is not possible, then there should be a break between exercises because this seems to be most favorable to perfecting technique. Unless there is no other way, you should not train both the snatch and the clean and jerk in the same workout. Do not learn to snatch like you clean, as both exercises are different and this can limit potential (2, 6).

It should be noted that competition lifts are not done very often in weightlifting programs. Generally competition lifts are only performed every 7-10 days (6, 9, 10). The reason for this is that it seems that those lifters that train with the competition lifts more often also seem to have more days of training lost due to injury. This is probably due to the fact that these lifts are very technique-intensive and when lifters get tired, technique will slip, causing injury (10).

Power cleans and power snatches (from the floor, from the hang, and from blocks) should form the backbone of training. These movements are performed at speeds that are faster than the competition lifts so they help to develop speed and technique (9).

Generally, it is recommended that lifters do 3-8 exercises per workout (6).

Exercise Order

Weightlifting workouts should follow this pattern:

1. Warm up
2. Speed exercises - i.e. snatch, clean, jerk
3. Strength exercises - i.e. squats, pulls, presses, bend overs
4. Endurance exercises - jumps, plyometrics, sprints
5. Flexibility work (4, 6, 9)

The most complicated exercises should be done first in a workout when you are still fresh. Not only will fatigue reduce the effectiveness of the training, it can also increase the likelihood of getting injured, especially with the competition lifts (10).

For example, if you were going to perform exercises from every category that has been listed above in one workout (which is **not** recommended, by the way), the exercise order would be:

1. Snatch combination
2. Snatch
3. Clean and Jerk combination
4. Clean and Jerk
5. Pulls
6. Squats
7. Presses
8. Bend Overs

Snatch combination exercises are the most complicated and strenuous exercises, so they are performed first. The snatch follows, as this is also complicated and strenuous (however not as bad as snatch + overhead squats, or something similar). Next come clean and jerk combination work, then the clean and jerk exercises. Pulls, squats, presses, and bend overs finish out the "workout." Bend overs should be performed last - this is because you need your lower back muscles to perform all of the exercises listed above.

Periodization Basics

Periodization refers to the cycling of training in order to help the lifter peak for competition. In a periodized training plan, the year is broken down into training blocks where exercises employed, volume, intensity, rest, etc. are all manipulated.

It should be kept in mind that the primary goal in a weightlifting training program is to allow the lifter to be at their best for competition. All other goals are subordinate to that. When designing a training program one must ask these questions: Will this improve my snatch? Will this improve my clean and jerk? Weightlifting training is organized around improving those two lifts.

A weightlifter's training is organized into blocks. There are three levels of these blocks:

1. Macrocycles
2. Mesocycles
3. Microcycles

Macrocycles

Macrocycles are the largest block of training in a periodized program. Generally they refer to an entire year, although in some cases they may refer to a four year period or there may even be several macrocycles in a year (6). This book will use three macrocycles per twelve month period.

Mesocycles

Several mesocycles make up a macrocycle. These are phases lasting several weeks that are designed to accomplish specific objectives (i.e. improve strength/power, increase hypertrophy, etc.). There are four types of mesocycles that are used in this book (although different periodization models utilize different types of mesocycles):

1. General Preparation
2. Special Preparation
3. Competition
4. Transitional (11, 12)

The *general preparation* mesocycle is designed to increase the lifter's fitness (9, 12). This cycle is designed to accomplish a number of objectives: develop hypertrophy, increase strength, increase endurance, and improve technical skill on the lifts. The general preparation phase is the basic foundation for achieving technical mastery and for achieving the maximal effects from training (12). A wide variety of exercises are utilized to accomplish the objectives of the general preparation phase with moderate volume and intensity (6).

The *special preparation* mesocycle is designed to apply the fitness that the lifter develops in the general phase to the skills that the lifter needs for weightlifting (i.e. speed-strength). Overall fitness is maintained, but now the workouts specifically target speed-strength, the competition lifts, and technique (9, 13). The choice of exercises is restricted somewhat to focus on maintenance, technique and speed-strength (6). Volume and intensity will be varied (depending on the exercise) when compared to the general preparation phase. Generally, intensity will increase on the competition exercises (13).

The *competition* mesocycle is designed to peak the lifter for an upcoming competition, consolidate sports skills, and maintain fitness. In this phase extraneous exercises are removed from the program to allow the lifter to concentrate on furthering their strength and skills in the competition lifts (6, 9, 14). Volume on the competition lifts, pulls, and squats may increase in this phase (relative to the total amount of work done) but overall number of lifts will decrease as intensity increases. Usually the heaviest work will be done in the competition phase (14).

The *transitional* mesocycle is a period to allow the lifter to recover. This phase utilizes active rest to keep the lifter in shape while allowing muscles and joints to recover from the previous training (9, 15). It is important to note that a lifter does not stop training while in the transitional period, they merely utilize different exercises and different methods of training to provide variety and allow recovery. Volume and intensity are both very low during this phase. The lifter still trains, but at a greatly reduced pace.

Microcycles
Microcycles are the smallest division of the training plan. Generally they last a week (6, 11).

Different training blocks require different approaches to training. For example, during the general phase the lifter may be performing a number of slow, controlled exercises such as squats, deadlifts, and lunges to build up some strength and hypertrophy. However, in the special phase the lifter will begin to perform jumps and other explosive exercises to transfer that strength and hypertrophy to weightlifting. In addition; volume, intensity, and even rest are manipulated in each phase of training to produce different results (this is all covered in more detail in chapters seven and eight).

Warming Up and Flexibility

Warming up and flexibility work are often overlooked components of a weightlifter's training. Both these components are important for injury prevention and for maximizing performance (3, 4).

Warming Up

The warm up is designed to prepare the body for work. It is divided into two phases; the general warm-up and the activity specific warm-up (1, 3, 4).

The *general warm-up* is designed to elevate the heart rate gradually and get blood circulating into the muscles and joints (especially those muscles and joints that will be exercised) (1, 4). In weightlifting, a general warm-up will include exercises like jogging, walking bouncing steps on the toes, duck walks, lunges, twisting, arm circles, jumping exercises, etc. (2, 3). Some authors recommend performing sets of hyperextensions and abdominal work in addition to jumping exercises during the warm-up (5). The general warm-up should last for 10-15 minutes and should consist of 10-12 exercises (like the ones mentioned above) performed 6-8 times each (3).

The *activity specific warm-up* is designed to prepare the body for the specific movements it will be performing. The activity specific warm-up should focus on those joints and muscles that will be trained during the workout. In weightlifting, an activity specific warm up would involve starting out with light weights and progressing slowly to the workout weights (1, 4).

Flexibility

Flexibility is important not only for injury prevention but also because it helps the lifter master technique faster (7). A weightlifter should focus their flexibility work on several joints: shoulders, lower back, hips, and the ankles. One word of caution about flexibility work; do not stretch a "cold" muscle. Always make sure to stretch after the warm-up. Cold muscles are more easily injured and stretching cold muscles can result in injury (4).

References:

1. Allerheiligen, W.B. (1994). Stretching and warm-up. In Baechle, T.R. (Ed.). Essentials of Strength Training and Conditioning (pp. 289-313). Champaign, Il: Human Kinetics.
2. Frolov, V.I., & A.A. Lukashev. (1978). A comparative analysis of snatch and clean technique. Tyazhelaya Atletika, 26-28. Translated by Yesis, M. (1979). Soviet Sports Review, 14(2), 80-82.
3. Gavatsko, S.P., & A.R. Rabzievsky. (1980). Rational make-up of the general-warmup in training and competition. In Lelikov, S.I., A.S. Medvedev, Y.S. Povetkin, P.A. Poletayev, R.A. Roman, Y.A. Sandalov, & A.V. Chernyak (Eds.). 1980 Weightlifting Yearbook (pp. 76-80. Moscow: Fizkultura I Sport. Translated by Charniga, Jr., A. (1986). Livonia, Michigan: Sportivny Press.
4. Jones, L. (1991). USWF Coaching Accreditation Course Club Coach Manual. Colorado Springs, CO.: U.S. Weightlifting Federation, 9-12, 64-69.
5. Medvedev, A.S. (1980). Periodization of training in weightlifting (The plan of preparation for a base meso-cycle). In Lelikov, S.I., A.S. Medvedev, Y.S. Povetkin, P.A. Poletayev, R.A. Roman, Y.A. Sandalov, & A.V. Chernyak (Eds.). 1980 Weightlifting Yearbook (pp. 16-25). Moscow: Fizkultura I Sport. Translated by Charniga, Jr., A. (1986). Livonia, Michigan: Sportivny Press.
6. Medvedyev, A.S. (1986). A System of Multi-Year Training in Weightlifting. Moscow: Fizkultura I Sport. Translated by Charniga, Jr., A. (1989). Livonia, Michigan: Sportivny Press, 60-84, 102-138, 154, 166, 172.

7. Moroz, R.P. (1992). Improving flexibility (mobility) with the aid of resistance. Weightlifting Training and Technique. Translated by Charniga, Jr., A. Livonia, Michigan: Sportivny Press.

8. Rodionov, V.I. (1976). Number of repetitions per set in lifting exercises. Tyazhelaya Atletika, 24-26. Translated by Yesis, M. (1979). Soviet Sports Review, 14(3), 114-116.

9. Roman, R.A. (1986). The Training of the Weightlifter. Moscow: Fizkultura I Sport. Translated by Charniga, Jr., A. Livonia, Michigan: Sportivny Press, 41-48, 78-106, 156.

10. Stone, M.H., A.C. Fry, M. Ritchie, L. Stoessel-Ross, & J.L. Marsit. (1994). Injury potential and safety aspects of weightlifting movements. Strength and Conditioning, 16(3), 15-21.

11. Yesis, M. (1982). Trends in Soviet strength and conditioning - From macro to meso to micro-cycles. NSCA Journal, 4(4), 45-47.

12. Yesis, M. (1982). Trends in Soviet strength and conditioning - The role of all-around, general physical preparation in the multiyear and yearly training programs. NSCA Journal, 4(5), 48-50.

13. Yesis, M. (1983). Trends in Soviet strength and conditioning - The role of specialized training in multiyear and yearly training programs. NSCA Journal, 4(6), 10-11, 36.

14. Yesis, M. (1983). Trends in Soviet strength and conditioning - The competitive period in the multiyear and yearly training programs. NSCA Journal, 5(1), 45-46.

15. Yesis, M. (1983). Trends in Soviet strength and conditioning - The transitional period. NSCA Journal, 5(2), 64-65.

16. Vorobyev, A.N. (1978). The scientific basis of weightlifting training and technique. Teoriya I Praktika Fizicheskoi Kultury, 5, 8-11. Translated by Yesis, M. (1979). Soviet Sports Review, 14(1), 1-5.

Chapter Seven
Program Design for Beginners

<table>
<tr><td colspan="2">Chapter Outline:</td></tr>
<tr><td>

What is a beginner?
How the training year is broken down
The First Macrocycle
  Transitional Mesocycle
  General Preparation Mesocycle
  Special Preparation Mesocycle
  Competition Mesocycles

</td><td>

The Second Macrocycle
The Third Macrocycle
  Transitional Mesocycle
  General Preparation Mesocycle
  Special Preparation Mesocycle
  Competition Mesocycles

</td></tr>
</table>

Chapter Objectives:

1. Understand what goes into the designing of programs for beginners
2. Understand how to organize training into macrocycles and mesocycles
3. Understand how to manipulate exercise selection, volume, and intensity in each mesocycle

For purposes of this book, a beginner is someone who either has just begun training in the sport or someone who has not yet qualified for a national-level competition. This chapter deals with the training of an absolute beginner (i.e. someone brand new to the sport). The training of beginners revolves around several things:

- Developing the lifter's fitness
- Developing proper technique
- Preparing the lifter for competition by giving them experience

Because this is a beginner, assistance exercises are emphasized during their training - in order to develop their muscles and joints. While they are still performed at the intermediate level, they do not make up as great a percentage of the whole when compared to beginners. Two other additional points should be made about the beginner's training: first, beginners are *not* trained at a percentage of their 1-RM. This is because a beginner will not have good enough technique to have a consistent 1-RM. Lifters should employ the most weight that they can handle, for a specified number of repetitions, with correct technique, *for that day.* Second, every repetition a beginner performs counts towards the NL. With more advanced lifters only reps performed over a certain percentage of 1-RM are counted towards the total NL - so warm up sets do count with beginners.

In this book, there are three major national-level competitions each year that lifters prepare for; Collegiate Nationals (in October), the American Open (in November or December) and Nationals (March or April). From the very beginning of a lifter's training, they should be trained to peak for those meets *even if they won't actually get to those meets for several years.*

With this in mind, the beginner's training is organized around three macrocycles: the first macrocycle runs from the day after Nationals through the Collegiate Nationals. The second macrocycle runs from the day after the Collegiate Nationals through the American Open. The third runs from the day after the American Open through Nationals. For purposes of this book we will use the 1997/1998 competition calendar. The lengths of the macrocycles are in table 7-1.

Macrocycle	Start Date	End Date	Length (weeks)
First	28 April 1997	11 Oct 1997	24
Second	12 Oct 1997	9 Nov 1997	4
Second	10 Nov 1997	6 April 1998	21

Table 7-1: Macrocycle Lengths for Beginners

The following sections will discuss in general how the macrocycles / mesocycles are organized. They will go into detail on each of the macrocycles, explain how exercise selection, volume, and intensity should be manipulated.

The First Macrocycle

The first macrocycle runs from 21 April 1997 through the Collegiate Nationals, which ends on 11 October 1997. It lasts a total of 24 weeks. Please note, that this macrocycle is laid out to apply to absolute beginners - so some things may be different for a more "experienced" beginner. Once the length of the macrocycle has been determined, it's time to break it down into mesocycles. Remember that there are four types: general preparation, special preparation, competition, and transitional. This is achieved by deciding when the lifter will be competing during the macrocycle and then moving backwards.

The most important meet of the macrocycle that the lifter should be preparing for is Collegiate Nationals, on 11 October. Six weeks prior to that a prepatory meet should be held to evaluate the lifter's current level of development, this allows changes to be made in training to address any deficiencies before Collegiates. This prepatory meet also gives them a chance to qualify for Collegiates. This meet is held six weeks out to give lifters a chance to participate in another meet if they do not lift well in this one and qualify. Ten weeks prior to the prepatory meet a developmental meet should be held to get the lifter used to standing in front of people and lifting. It is very important that beginners get used to competing from the very start of their training.

> Using the above guidelines, the competition schedule for the first macrocycle is:
> Developmental Meet   21 June 1997
> Prepatory Meet   30 August 1997
> National Collegiates   11 October 1997

The period from 30 August and 11 October will be classified as a competition mesocycle, as will the period from 17 August to 30 August (i.e. 2 weeks before the Prepatory Meet). Note that the lifter will not enter a competition mesocycle for the developmental meet as this meet is seen as a part of the lifter's training.

> Competition mesocycle schedule for macrocycle one:
> Competition I   17 August to 30 August 1997
> Competition II   31 August to 11 October 1997

The special prepatory mesocycle that will last eight weeks. This phase will run from 22 June 1997 to 16 August 1997. Note that the special preparation cycle starts right after the developmental meet. The developmental meet will give the coach a chance to see what qualities the lifter needs to concentrate on in the special preparation cycle.

The period from 11 May 1997 to 21 June 1997 will form the general prepatory mesocycle. Finally, the two weeks after Nationals (i.e. 28 April to 10 May) will form the transitional mesocycle.

The entire breakdown of the first macrocycle can be seen in table 7-2.

Mesocycle	Start Date	End Date	Length (weeks)
Transitional	28 April 1997	10 May 1997	2
General Preparation	11 May 1997	21 June 1997	6
Developmental Meet	21 June 1997		
Special Preparation	22 June 1997	16 August 1997	8
Competition I	17 August 1997	30 August 1997	2
Prepatory Meet	30 August 1997		
Competition II	31 August 1997	11 October 1997	6
National Collegiates	11 October 1997		

Table 7-2: First macrocycle breakdown

The Transitional Mesocycle

Recall that the purpose of the transitional mesocycle is to allow the lifter a chance to recover from the previous macrocycle's training. This is achieved by a reduction in volume and intensity as well as a focus away from the competition movements. Lifters should not train more than six times during this two week mesocycle. Some suggestions for exercises to include in this mesocycle, by exercise category (see chapter six for exercise categories) are listed below:

Snatch exercises: Power snatch.

Snatch combination exercises: No exercises from this category.

Clean and Jerk exercises: Power clean.

Clean and Jerk combination exercises: No exercises from this category.

Squats: Back squats and front squats.

Pulls: No exercises from this category.

Bend Overs: Hyperextensions.

Presses: Military press (seated).

This means a total of 6 exercises are planned for the transitional mesocycle. Workouts should be broken down as follows:

Workout One: Snatch, squats, bend overs
Workout Two: Clean, squats, presses
Workout Three: Squats, bend overs, presses

Table 7-3 describes the set and rep scheme for the exercises in this phase of training.

Exercise Category	Number of Sets / Exercise	Number of Reps / Set
Snatch	3	4
Cleans	3	4
Squats	3	10
Bend Overs	3	6
Presses	3	6

Table 7-3: Set and rep breakdown by exercise category for the transitional phase of the first macrocycle.

In the transitional phase, not only are the sets and reps reduced to make the workouts easy, but the exercises available for training are restricted to give the lifter a chance to recover. The idea is to maintain motor skills.

General Preparation Mesocycle

The purpose of the general preparation mesocycle is to develop the lifter's fitness. This is achieved by using a wide variety of exercises with a moderate amount of volume and intensity. Lifters will train 3 days per week in this phase, so this mesocycle will have a total of 18 workouts. Normally one would not train both the snatch and the clean and jerk in the same workout - however this phase is only designed to teach the basics of both lifts while developing every aspect of the lifter's fitness. Note that the competition lifts (i.e. classic snatch and classic clean) are not trained during this mesocycle. Some Soviet coaches recommend waiting up to 2-3 years before training the classic lifts (7). While this would work in an ideal situation (i.e. very young lifters in a controlled environment) this will probably not be practical in America. As a result, classic work will begin in the special preparation phase. This phase is designed to teach the skills necessary to learn the classic lifts (explosiveness, balance, etc.). Also note that exercises from the hang are not taught during the entire first year of training. This is due to the fact that lifters need a certain amount of strength and technical mastery to get the full benefit of performing exercises from the hang (7). In order to develop both (and to provide variety) exercises are performed from blocks instead. Beginners will not perform pulls during this cycle, the work they perform on the power snatch/ power clean will suffice. Once again, beginners will not train at a percentage of their 1-RM, rather they should train at the most weight they can handle, correctly, for the specified number of repetitions *on that day*.

Some suggestions for exercises to include in this mesocycle, by exercise category are listed below:

Snatch exercises: Power snatch, power snatch from blocks (above and below the knee), and overhead squats.

Snatch combination exercises: Power snatch + overhead squats (from the floor and from blocks).

Clean and Jerk exercises: Power clean, power clean from blocks (above and below the knee), push jerk, and split jerk.

Clean and Jerk combination exercises: Power clean + push jerk (from the floor and from blocks), power clean + split jerk (from the floor and from blocks).

Squats: Back squats and front squats.

Pulls: No exercises from this category.

Bend Overs: Hyperextensions and good mornings (standing).

Presses: Military press and behind the neck press (snatch grip).

This means a total of 24 exercises are planned for the general preparation mesocycle. Workouts should be broken down, by week, as follows:

Workout One: Snatch exercises, clean and jerk exercises, squats, bend overs
Workout Two: Snatch exercises, clean and jerk exercises, squats, presses
Workout Three: Snatch combination exercises, clean and jerk combination exercises, squats

Table 7-4 describes the set and rep scheme for the exercises in this phase of training.

Exercise Category	Sets / Exercise	Reps / Set
Snatch Exercises	3-5	2-4
Snatch Combination Exercises	3-5	1-4
Clean and Jerk Exercises	3-5	2-4
Clean and Jerk Combination Exercises	3-5	1-4
Squats	3	4-10
Bend Overs	3	6-10
Presses	3	6-10

Table 7-4: Set and rep breakdown by exercise category for the general preparation phase of the first macrocycle.

Keep in mind that this phase is meant to introduce the lifter to training for weightlifting and to develop the lifter's fitness level.

A sample workout for the general preparation phase follows, included are the NL for each week.

Week One

Workout #1:

1.	Power snatch	4x4
2.	Push Jerk, racks	4x4
3.	Back squats	3x10
4.	Hyperextensions	3x10

Total NL Workout #1: 92

Workout #2:

1.	Power snatch, b, AK	4x4
2.	Split Jerk	4x3
3.	Front Squats	3x10
4.	Military Press	3x10

Total NL Workout #2: 88

Workout #3:

1.	Power Snatch, b, BK + Overhead squat	3x3+2
2.	Power Clean + Push Jerk	3x3+2
3.	Back Squats	3x8

Total NL Workout #3: 54
Total NL for Week One: 234

Week Two

Workout #4:

1.	Overhead Squats	4x4
2.	Power Clean, b, AK	4x4
3.	Front Squats	3x10
4.	Good Mornings, Standing	3x10

Total NL Workout #4: 92

Workout #5:

1.	Power Snatch	4x4
2.	Power Clean, b, BK	4x4
3.	Back Squats	3x10
4.	BNP, Snatch grip	3x10

Total NL Workout #5: 92

Workout #6:

1.	Power Snatch, b, AK + Overhead Squats	3x3+2
2.	Power Clean + Split Jerk	3x3+2
3.	Front Squats	3x8

Total NL Workout #6: 54
Total NL for Week Two: 238

Week Three

Workout #7:

1.	Power Snatch, b, BK	4x3
2.	Power Clean, b, AK	4x3
3.	Back Squats	3x8
4.	Good Mornings, Standing	3x8

Total NL Workout #7: 72

Workout #8:

1.	Overhead Squats	4x3
2.	Power Clean, b, BK	4x3
3.	Front Squats	3x8
4.	Military Press	3x8

Total NL Workout #8: 72

Workout #9:

1.	Power Snatch + Overhead Squats	2x3+2, 2x2+1
2.	Power Clean + Push Jerk	2x3+2, 2x2+1
3.	Back Squats	3x6

Total NL Workout #9: 50
Total NL Week Three: 194

Week Four

Workout #10:

1.	Power Snatch, b, AK	4x3
2.	Power Clean, b, AK	4x3
3.	Front Squats	3x8
4.	Hyperextensions	3x8

Total NL Workout #10: 72

Workout #11:

1.	Power Snatch, b, BK	4x3
2.	Power Clean, b, BK	4x3
3.	Back Squats	3x8
4.	Behind the Neck Press, Snatch Grip	3x8

Total NL Workout #11: 72

Workout #12:

1.	Power Snatch + Overhead Squats	2x3+2, 2x2+1
2.	Power Clean + Push Jerk	2x3+2, 2x2+1
3.	Front Squats	3x6

Total NL Workout #12: 50
Total NL Week Four: 194

Starting with week 5 lifters begin to transition to the special preparation phase and learning the combination lifts. As a result the combination exercises are now performed every other workout.

Week Five
Workout #13:
1. Overhead Squats   5x2
2. Split Jerk   5x2
3. Back Squats   3x6
4. Good Mornings, Standing 3x6
Total NL Workout #13: 56

Workout #14:
1. Power Snatch + Overhead
   Squats   5x2+1
2. Power Clean + Split Jerk
   5x2+1
3. Front Squats   3x4
4. Military Press   3x4
Total NL Workout #14: 54

Workout #15:
1. Power Snatch, b, AK   5x2
2. Power Clean, b, AK   5x2
3. Back Squats   3x6
Total NL Workout #15: 38
Total NL Week Five: 148

Week Six

Workout #16:
1. Power Snatch, b, BK +
   Overhead Squats   5x2+1
2. Power Clean, b, BK + Split Jerk
   5x2+1
3. Front Squats   3x4
4. Hyperextensions   3x4
Total NL Workout #16: 54

Workout #17:
1. Overhead Squats   5x2
2. Push Jerk   5x2
3. Back Squats   3x6
4. Behind the Neck Press, Snatch
   Grip   3x6
Total NL Workout #17: 56

Workout #18:
1. Power Snatch + Overhead
   Squats   5x2+1
2. Power Clean + Split Jerk
   5x2+1
3. Front Squats   3x4
Total NL Workout #18: 42
Total NL Week Six: 152

Total NL General Preparation Mesocycle: 1160

A word on notation. Power Snatch, b, AK refers to the power snatch from blocks, with the bar starting above the knees. BK refers to below the knees. The set/rep schemes are written in the following format: # of sets x # of reps per set. Power clean, b, AK + Split jerk at 4x2+2 refers to performing 4 sets of 2 cleans and then 2 jerks.

Table 7-5 shows the breakdown of NL by the major exercises for the general preparation mesocycle described above.

Exercises	NL from Category	% of Total NL
Snatch Exercises	249	21.5%
Clean and Jerk Exercises	249	21.5%
Squats	390	33.6%
Bend Overs	134	11.6%
Presses	138	11.9%

Table 7-5: Percentage of total NL for general preparation mesocycle, based on the workouts shown in text.

Special Preparation Mesocycle

The purpose of the special preparation mesocycle is to apply the lifter's fitness to weightlifting. More work is spent developing technique and speed-strength. As a result, the competition lifts are introduced while some of the assistance work is minimized by comparison.

In order to aid with this, pulls are introduced into this phase. Volume and intensity are increased on the snatch, clean and jerk, squats, and pulls while it is maintained or reduced on the bend overs and presses. In this phase of the first macrocycle, lifters will train four times per week. Two workouts will be geared to the snatch, two to the clean and jerk.

Some suggestions for exercises to include in this mesocycle, by exercise category are listed below:

Snatch exercises: Classic snatch, classic snatch from blocks, power snatch, overhead squats, and snatch balance.

Snatch combination exercises: Classic snatch + overhead squats (from the floor and from blocks).

Clean and Jerk exercises: Classic clean, classic clean from blocks, power clean, squat jerk, and split jerk.

Clean and Jerk combination exercises: Classic clean + split jerk (from the floor and from blocks).

Squats: Back squats and front squats.

Pulls: Snatch pulls from the blocks (above and below the knee), clean pulls from blocks (above and below the knee).

Bend Overs: Hyperextensions, good mornings (standing), and Romanian deadlifts.

Presses: Military press, behind the neck press (snatch grip), and push press (snatch grip).

This means a total of 30 exercises are planned for the special preparation mesocycle. Workouts should be broken down as follows:

Workout One: Snatch exercises, pulls, front squats
Workout Two: Clean and jerk exercises, pulls, back squats
Workout Three: Snatch combination exercises, front squats, bend overs
Workout Four: Clean and jerk combination exercises, back squats, presses

Table 7-6 describes the set and rep scheme for the exercises in this phase of training.

Exercise Category	Sets / Exercise	Reps / Set
Snatch Exercises	5-7	2-4
Snatch Combination Exercises	3-7	1-4
Clean and Jerk Exercises	5-7	2-4
Clean and Jerk Combination Exercises	3-7	1-4
Squats	3	2-8
Pulls	3	2-4
Bend Overs	3	2-6
Presses	3	2-6

Table 7-6: Set and rep breakdown by exercise category for the special preparation phase of the first macrocycle.

A sample workout for the special preparation phase follows, NL is included for each week.

Week One
Workout #1:
1. Classic Snatch   5x4
2. Snatch Pulls, b, AK   3x4
3. Front Squats   3x8

Workout #2:
1. Split Jerk   5x4
2. Clean Pulls, b, AK   3x4
3. Back Squats   3x8

Workout #3:
1. Classic Snatch, b, AK + Overhead
   Squats   5x3+2
2. Front Squats   3x6
3. Hyperextensions   3x6

Workout #4:
1. Classic Clean + Split Jerk   5x3+2
2. Back Squats   3x6
3. Military Press   3x6
Total NL Week One: 234

Week Two
Workout #5:
1. Classic Snatch, b, BK   6x3
2. Snatch Pulls, b, BK   3x4
3. Front Squats   3x6

Workout #6:
1. Classic Clean, b, AK   6x3
2. Clean Pulls, b, BK   3x4
3. Back Squats   3x6

Workout #7:
1. Power Snatch + Overhead Squats
   6x2+1
2. Front Squats   3x4
3. Good Mornings, Standing   3x6

Workout #8:
1. Classic Clean, b, BK + Split Jerk 6x2+1
2. Back Squats   3x4
3. Military Press   3x6
Total NL Week Two: 192

Week Three
Workout #9:
1. Snatch Balance   6x3
2. Snatch Pulls, b, AK   3x4
3. Front Squats   3x6

Workout #10:
1. Squat Jerk   6x3
2. Clean Pulls, b, AK   3x4
3. Back Squats   3x6

Workout #11:
1. Classic Snatch + Overhead Squats
   6x2+1
2. Front Squats   3x4
3. Romanian Deadlifts   3x4

Workout #12:
1. Power Clean + Split Jerk   6x2+1
2. Back Squats   3x4
3. Behind the Neck Press, Snatch Grip 3x4
Total NL Week Three: 188

Week Four
Workout #13:
1. Classic Snatch, b, AK   6x3
2. Snatch Pulls, b, BK   3x4
3. Front Squats   3x6

Workout #14:
1. Classic Clean   6x3
2. Clean Pulls, b, BK   3x4
3. Back Squats   3x6

Workout #15:
1. Classic Snatch, b, BK + Overhead
   Squats   6x2+1
2. Front Squats   3x4
3. Hyperextensions   3x4

Workout #16:
1. Classic Clean, b, AK + Squat Jerk
   6x2+1
2. Back Squats   3x4
3. Push Press, Snatch Grip   3x4
Total NL Week Four: 188

Week Five
Workout #17:
1. Snatch Balance   6x3
2. Snatch Pulls, b, AK   3x4
3. Front Squats   3x6

Workout #18:
1. Classic Clean, b, BK   6x3
2. Clean Pulls, b, AK   3x4
3. Back Squats   3x6

Workout #19:
1. Power Snatch + Overhead Squats
   6x2+1
2. Front Squats   3x4
3. Good Mornings, Standing   3x4

Workout #20:
1. Power Clean + Split Jerk   6x2+1
2. Back Squats   3x4
3. Military Press   3x4
Total NL Week Five: 188

Week Six
Workout #21:
1. Classic Snatch   1x3, 3x2, 3x1
2. Snatch Pulls, b, BK   3x3
3. Front Squats   3x4

Workout #22:
1. Squat Jerk   1x3, 3x2, 3x1
2. Clean Pulls, b, BK 3x3
3. Back Squats   3x4

Workout #23:
1. Classic Snatch, b, AK + Overhead
   Squats   1x3+2, 3x2+1, 3x1+1
2. Front Squats   3x2
3. Romanian Deadlifts 3x2

Workout #24:
1. Classic Clean + Split Jerk   1x3+2,
   3x2+1, 3x1+1
2. Back Squats   3x2
3. Behind the Neck Press, Snatch Grip 3x2
Total NL Week Six: 134

Week Seven
Workout #25:
1. Classic Snatch, b, BK   1x3, 3x2,
   3x1
2. Snatch Pulls, b, AK   3x3
3. Front Squats   3x4

Workout #26:
1. Classic Clean, b, AK   1x3, 3x2,
   3x1
2. Clean Pulls, b, AK   3x3
3. Back Squats   3x4

Workout #27:
1. Power Snatch + Overhead Squats
   1x3+2, 3x2+1, 3x1+1
2. Front Squats   3x2
3. Hyperextensions   3x2

Workout #28:
1. Classic Clean, b, BK + Split Jerk 1x3+2,
   3x2+1, 3x1+1
2. Back Squats   3x2
3. Push Press, Snatch Grip   3x2
Total NL Week Seven: 134

Week Eight
Workout #29:
1. Snatch Balance   1x3, 2x2, 4x1
2. Snatch Pulls, b, BK   3x2
3. Front Squats   3x2

Workout #30:
1. Squat Jerk   1x3, 2x2, 4x1
2. Clean Pulls, b, BK 3x2
3. Back Squats   3x2

Workout #31:
1. Classic Snatch + Overhead Squats
   1x3+2, 1x2+1, 5x1+1
2. Front Squats   3x2
3. Good Mornings, Standing   3x2

Workout #32:
1. Power Clean + Split Jerk   1x3+2,
   1x2+1, 5x1+1
2. Back Squats   3x2
3. Military Press   3x2
Total NL Week Eight: 124

Total NL Special Preparation Mesocycle: 1382

Table 7-7 shows the breakdown of NL for the major exercises for the workout described above.

Exercises	NL from Category	% of Total NL
Snatch Exercises	282	20.4%
Clean and Jerk Exercises	282	20.4%
Squats	402	29.1%
Pulls	168	12.2%
Bend Overs	124	8.9%
Presses	124	8.9%

Table 7-7: Percentage of total NL for special preparation mesocycle, based on the workout shown in text.

Competition Mesocycle

The competition mesocycle is designed to bring everything together to allow the athlete to lift their best during competition. This phase of training sees the largest intensity, with a reduction in volume when compared to the other mesocycles. Assistance work is scaled back, the amount of time spent on snatches, clean and jerks, squats, and pulls is increased. During this mesocycle the athlete will be training five times a week (except for the week before competition, when the athlete will perform two workouts). The last heavy workout on the snatch should be performed no later than 7-9 days before competition, and the last heavy clean and jerk workout should be performed no later than 10-14 days before competition.

Some suggestions for exercises to include in this mesocycle, by exercise category (see chapter six for exercise categories) are listed below:

Snatch exercises: Classic snatch and power snatch.

Snatch combination exercises: Classic snatch + overhead squats.

Clean and Jerk exercises: Classic clean, power clean.

Clean and Jerk combination exercises: Classic clean + split jerk.

Squats: Back squats and front squats.

Pulls: Snatch pulls from the floor, snatch pulls from blocks (above and below the knee), clean pulls from the floor, clean pulls from blocks (above and below the knee).

Bend Overs: Hyperextensions, good mornings (standing), Romanian deadlifts.

Presses: Military press, behind the neck press (snatch grip).

This means a total of 19 exercises are planned for the special preparation mesocycle. Workouts should be broken down, by week, as follows:

Workout One: Snatch exercises, pulls, squats, bend overs (every 2nd week)
Workout Two: Clean and jerk exercises, pulls, squats, presses (every 2nd week)
Workout Three: Snatch combination exercises, pulls, squats
Workout Four: Clean and jerk combination exercises, pulls, squats
Workout Five: Snatch exercises, clean and jerk exercises

Table 7-8 describes the set and rep scheme for the exercises in this phase of training.

Exercise Category	Sets / Exercise	Reps / Set
Snatch Exercises	5-7	1-3
Snatch Combination Exercises	5-7	1-3
Clean and Jerk Exercises	5-7	1-3
Clean and Jerk Combination Exercises	5-7	1-3
Squats	3	2-6
Pulls	3-5	1-4
Bend Overs	3	2-6
Presses	3	2-6

Table 7-8: Set and rep breakdown by exercise category for the competition phase of the first macrocycle.

A sample workout for the competition I and competition II phases follows.

Competition I

Week One
Workout #1:
1. Classic Snatch   2x3, 4x2
2. Snatch Pulls   5x2
3. Back Squats   3x3

Workout #2:
1. Power Clean   2x3, 4x2
2. Clean Pulls   5x2
3. Front Squats   3x3

Workout #3:
1. Classic Snatch + Overhead Squats
2x3+2, 4x2+1
2. Snatch Pulls, b, AK   4x2
3 Back Squats   3x2

Workout #4:
1. Classic Clean + Split Jerk
   2x3+2, 4x2+1
2. Clean Pulls, b, AK   4x2
3. Front Squats   3x2

Workout #5:
1. Power Snatch   2x3, 4x2
2. Classic Clean   2x3, 4x2

Total NL Week One: 166

Week Two:
Workout #6:
1. Power Snatch   2x3, 2x2
2. Snatch Pulls, b, BK   4x2
3. Back Squats   3x4
4. Hyperextensions   3x4

Workout #7:
1. Power Clean   2x3, 2x2
2. Clean Pulls, b, BK   4x2
3. Front Squats   3x4
4. Military Press   3x4

Workout #8:
1. Classic Snatch   3x3
2. Classic Clean   3x3

Workout #9:
Off

Workout #10:
Developmental Meet

Total NL Week Two: 102
Total NL Competition I: 268

Competition II

Week One:
Workout #1:
1. Power Snatch   3x3, 2x2
2. Snatch Pulls   5x3
3. Back Squats   3x3

Workout #2:
1. Classic Clean   3x3, 2x2
2. Clean Pulls   5x3
3. Front Squats   3x3

Workout #3:
1. Classic Snatch + Overhead Squats
3x3+2, 2x2+1
2. Snatch Pulls, b, AK   3x3
3. Back Squats   3x2

Workout #4:
1. Classic Clean + Split Jerk
3x3+2, 2x2+1
2. Clean Pulls, b, AK   3x3
3. Front Squats   3x2

Workout #5:
1. Classic Snatch   3x3, 3x2
2. Power Clean   3x3, 3x2

Total NL Week One: 176

Week Two:
Workout #6:
1. Power Snatch   2x3, 3x2
2. Snatch Pulls, b, BK   4x2
3. Back Squats   3x2
4. Good Mornings, Standing   3x2

Workout #7:
1. Classic Clean   2x3, 3x2
2. Clean Pulls, b, BK   4x2
3. Front Squats   3x2
4. Push Press, Snatch Grip   3x2

Workout #8:
1. Classic Snatch + Overhead Squats
2x3+2, 3x2+1
2. Snatch Pulls   3x2
3. Back Squats   3x2

Workout #9:
1. Classic Clean + Split Jerk   2x3+2,
3x2+1
2   Clean Pulls   3x2
3   Front Squats   3x2

Workout #10:
1. Classic Snatch   2x3, 2x2, 2x1
2. Power Clean   2x3, 2x2, 2x1

Total NL Week Two: 150

Week Three:
Workout #11:
1. Power Snatch   2x3, 2x2, 3x1
2. Snatch Pulls, b, AK   3x2
3. Back Squats   3x2

Workout #12:
1. Classic Clean   2x3, 2x2, 3x1
2. Clean Pulls, b, AK   3x2
3. Front Squats   3x2

Workout #13:
1. Classic Snatch + Overhead Squats
2x3+2, 2x2+1, 3x1+1
2. Snatch Pulls, b, BK   3x2
3. Back Squats   3x2

Workout #14:
1. Classic Clean + Split Jerk   2x3+2,
2x2+1, 3x1+1
2. Clean Pulls, b, BK   3x2
3. Front Squats   3x2

Workout #15:
1. Classic Snatch   2x3, 1x2, 5x1
2. Power Clean   2x3, 1x2, 5x1

Total NL Week Three: 144

Week Four:
Workout #16:
1. Power Snatch   2x3, 2x2, 3x1
2. Snatch Pulls   3x2
3. Back Squats   3x2
4. Romanian Deadlifts 3x2

Workout #17:
1. Classic Clean   2x3, 2x2, 3x1
2. Clean Pulls   3x2
3. Front Squats   3x2
4. Push Press, Jerk Grip   3x2

Workout #18:
1. Classic Snatch + Overhead Squats
1x3+2, 2x2+1, 4x2+1
2. Snatch Pulls, b, AK   3x2
3. Back Squats   3x2

Workout #19:
1. Classic Clean + Split Jerk   1x3+2,
2x2+1, 4x2+1
2. Clean Pulls, b, AK   3x2
3. Front Squats   3x2

Workout #20:
1. Classic Snatch   4x2, 3x1
2. Power Clean   4x2, 3x1

Total NL Week Four: 180

Week Five:
Workout #21:
1. Power Snatch   7x3
2. Snatch Pulls, b, BK 3x3

Workout #22:
1. Classic Clean   7x3
2. Clean Pulls, b, BK   3x3

Workout #23:
1. Classic Snatch + Overhead Squats
          4x3+2
2. Snatch Pulls   3x2

Workout #24:
1. Classic Clean + Split Jerk   4x3+2
2. Clean Pulls   3x2

Workout #25:
1. Classic Snatch   7x3
2. Power Clean   7x3

Total NL Week Five: 154

Week Six:
Workout #26:
1. Power Snatch   3x3
2. Snatch Pulls, b, AK 3x3

Workout #27:
1. Classic Clean   3x3
2. Clean Pulls, b, AK   3x3

Workout #28:
Off

Workout #29:
Off

Workout #30:
Collegiate Nationals

Total NL Week Six: 36
Total NL Competition II: 840
Total NL Competition Phase: 1108
Total NL First Macrocycle of training: 3998

Table 7-9 shows the breakdown of NL for the major exercises for the competition phase described above.

Exercises	NL from Category	% of Total NL
Snatch Exercises	333	30%
Clean and Jerk Exercises	333	30%
Squats	156	14.1%
Pulls	218	19.6%
Bend Overs	24	2.2%
Presses	24	2.2%

Table 7-9: Percentage of total NL for competition mesocycles, based on the workout shown in text.

Table 7-10 breaks down the NL and % of Total NL for each category of exercise for the first macrocycle, running from the transitional phase through the competition phase.

Exercises	NL from Category	% of Total NL
Snatch Exercises	888	22.2%
Clean and Jerk Exercises	888	22.2%
Squats	1128	28.2%
Pulls	386	9.7%
Bend Overs	354	8.9%
Presses	354	8.9%

Table 7-10: Total NL and % of total NL for each exercise category during the first macrocycle, as described in the text.

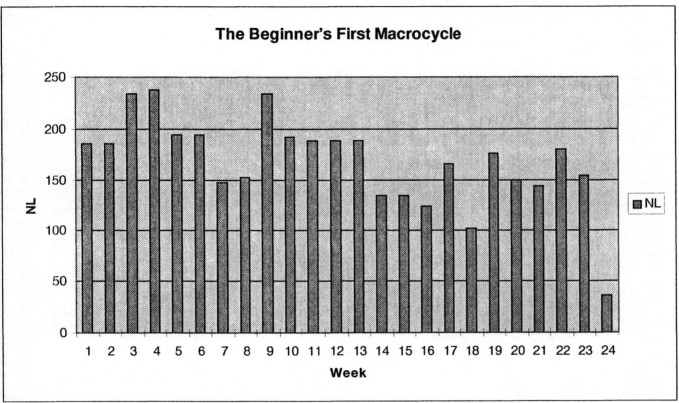

Figure 7-1: NL distribution by week for the first macrocycle, through competition II.

Figure 7-1 shows how the volume changes during the first macrocycle, from the transition mesocycle through competition II.

The Second Macrocycle

The second macrocycle is designed to peak the lifter for the American Open (7-9 Nov 1997). This meet is only four weeks after Collegiate Nationals which presents programming difficulties for a coach. The goal here is to improve the lifter's total while avoiding overtraining after the peaking process for Collegiate Nationals. As a result, the lifter's training will be broken down as follows:

Day One: Snatch exercises, snatch pulls, squats, bend overs (every 2nd week)
Day Two: Clean and jerk exercises, clean pulls, squats, presses (every 2nd week)
Day Three: Snatch exercises, snatch pulls, squats
Day Four: Clean + Jerk, clean pulls, squats
Day Five: Snatch exercises, clean and jerk exercises

Lifters will employ exercises from the following categories. Notice that with the exception of the clean + jerk, combination exercises are removed from the program:

Snatch exercises: Classic snatch and power snatch.

Clean and jerk exercises: Classic clean and power clean.

Clean and jerk combination exercises: Classic clean + split jerk.

Pulls: Snatch and clean pulls from the floor.

Squats: Front and back squats.

Presses: Military press.

Bend Overs: Good mornings, standing.

A total of 11 exercises are planned for this macrocycle of training.

With this training cycle, there isn't time to include a transitional phase. The first week of training (i.e. the week after Collegiate's) should be a reduced week - 3 sets/exercise with lighter weights. Weeks two and three should have an increased loading (i.e. regular 5-7 sets / fundamental exercise) with heavy weights. Week four (week of American Open) should only include 2-3 workouts with lighter weights.

The Third Macrocycle

This macrocycle is designed to peak the lifter for Nationals. The breakdown for this cycle can be seen in table 7-11.

Mesocycle	Start Date	End Date	Length (weeks)
Transitional I	10 November 1997	23 November 1997	2
Transitional II	24 November 1997	7 December 1997	2
General Preparation	8 December 1997	17 January 1998	6
Developmental Meet	17 January 1998		
Special Preparation	18 January 1998	21 February 1998	5
Prepatory Meet	21 February 1998		
Competition	22 February 1998	6 April 1998	6
Nationals	4-6 April 1998		

Table 7-11: Breakdown of the third macrocycle.

Transitional Mesocycles:
This training beings after the lifter has competed in the American Open. The lifter has completed 28 rigorous weeks of training without any real down time. For this period of training, there are two different transitional mesocycles. The first one introduces general training - to provide variety and expand the lifter's fitness; the second one gets the lifter back to performing the competition lifts.

Transitional I Mesocycle:
This mesocycle is designed to keep the lifter training, teach them new skills, and keep the lifter out of the weight room to allow for recovery. The lifter will be introduced to general training (GT) in this mesocycle, they should continue this type of training for the rest of their athletic career. GT has several categories of exercises:
1. Sprints: examples - 20, 40, 100 yards, etc.
2. Jumps: examples - standing broad jumps, vertical jumps, depth jumps, etc.
3. Misc. Exercises: examples - shot put, discus, swimming, etc.

Because this is the lifter's first exposure to performing these exercises systematically, and because the lifter needs a chance to allow their lower body to recover from the previous 24 weeks of training, squats are eliminated from their program during the transitional I mesocycle.

In addition to GT, lifters will perform exercises from the following categories:

Bend overs: Hyperextensions, good mornings (standing).

Presses: Military press, behind the neck press (snatch grip).

During this mesocycle, training will be broken down as follows:

> Day One: GT
> Day Two: Bend overs, presses
> Day Three: GT

As with all transitional phases, volume and intensity are low - lifters should perform 3 sets of 4 reps/exercise with very light and easy weights. A sample one-week program follows:

Transitional I Mesocycle, sample

Week One:
Workout 1 (GT):
1. 1x250, slow (warm up)
2. Stretching
3. 3x40 yards
4. 1x80 yards
5. Vertical jump (with counter movement)
      20 total

Workout #2:
1. Hyperextensions   3x4
2. Military Press   3x4

Workout #3:
1. 1x250, slow (warm up)
2. Stretching
3. 4x40 yards
4. 2x80 yards
5. 1x100 yards
6. Broad jump with 2-3 running steps   20 total

Transitional II Mesocycle:
This cycle continues to promote active recovery and begins to get the lifter used to training the Olympic lifts. Squats and the Olympic lifts are gradually integrated with the GT starting with this phase.

Lifters will employ exercises from the following categories during this phase of training:

Snatch exercises: Power snatch.

Clean and Jerk exercises: Power clean, push jerk.

Squats: Front squats, back squats.

Bend overs: Hyperextensions, good mornings (standing).

Presses: Military press, behind the neck press (snatch grip).

Workouts are broken down as follows:

Day One: Snatch exercises, squats, bend overs
Day Two: Clean and jerk exercises, squats, presses
Day Three: GT

Once again, volume is kept to 3 sets/exercise, with 4 reps/ set. The weights should be light and easy (the focus should be on technique).

General Preparation Mesocycle:

This phase lasts 6 weeks. As before, the idea is to develop the lifter's all-around fitness. Lifters will train 4 days/week, but only 3 days will be devoted to weights - the 4th day will be a GT day. This is done to continue to develop speed and explosiveness. It also provides variety. The competition movements are performed every 3rd workout, however the focus is on "power" movements (i.e. power snatch, power clean, etc.). In addition, combination lifts are only performed every 3rd workout. The sets and reps break down like in table 7-4.

Some suggestions for exercises to include in this mesocycle, by exercise category (see chapter six for exercise categories) are listed below:

Snatch exercises: Classic snatch, power snatch, power snatch from blocks (above and below the knee), overhead squats.

Snatch combination exercises: Classic snatch + overhead squats, snatch pulls + power snatch (from the floor, from blocks).

Clean and jerk exercises: Classic clean, power clean, power clean from blocks (above and below the knee), push jerk, split jerk.

Clean and jerk combination exercises: Classic clean + split jerk, power clean + split jerk (from the floor, from blocks).

Squats: Front squats and back squats.

Pulls: Snatch pulls (from the floor), clean pulls (from the floor).

Bend overs: Good mornings (standing), good mornings (seated), Romanian deadlifts

Presses: Military press, behind the neck press (snatch grip).

Workouts for the general preparation mesocycle should be broken down as follows:

Day One: Snatch exercise, clean and jerk exercise, pulls, squats
Day Two: Snatch exercise, clean and jerk exercise, squats, bend overs
Day Three: Snatch combination exercise, clean and jerk combination exercise, squats,
            presses
Day Four: GT

Special Preparation Mesocycle:

This phase lasts 5 weeks and still seeks to apply the lifter's fitness to the sport of Olympic lifting. Lifters will train 4 days/week during this phase. Once again, speed movements are introduced and the competition lifts are prioritized as assistance work is gradually phased out. GT is integrated with the weight workouts, although it is only performed once every other week. For set and rep suggestions, see table 7-6.

Some suggestions for exercises to include in this mesocycle, by exercise category (see chapter six for exercise categories) are listed below:

Snatch exercises: Classic snatch, classic snatch from blocks (above and below the knee), power snatch, snatch balance.

Snatch combination exercises: Classic snatch + overhead squats (from the floor and from blocks), snatch pulls + classic snatch (from the floor, from blocks).

Clean and jerk exercises: Classic clean, classic clean from blocks (above and below the knee), power clean, squat jerk, split jerk.

Clean and jerk combination exercises: Classic clean + split jerk (from the floor, from blocks), classic clean + front squat (from the floor, from blocks).

Squats: Front squats and back squats.

Pulls: Snatch pulls (from the floor and from blocks), clean pulls (from the floor and from blocks).

Bend overs: Good mornings (standing), good mornings (seated), Romanian deadlifts.

Presses: Military press, push press (snatch grip), push press (jerk grip).

Workouts for the special preparation mesocycle should be broken down as follows:

> Day One: Snatch exercise, pulls, squats, bend overs (GT once every other week, when GT is employed do not perform squats)
> Day Two: Clean and jerk exercise, pulls, squats presses
> Day Three: Snatch combination exercise, pulls, squats
> Day Four: Clean and jerk combination exercise, pulls, squats

Competition Mesocycle:

This phase lasts 6 weeks and is designed to peak the lifter for Nationals. Except for the week of Nationals, lifters will train 5 days/week. For set and rep suggestions, see table 7-8. GT is removed from the lifter's training, to allow more focus on the competition lifts. In addition, assistance work is almost completely phased out unless it is needed - presses and bend overs are not performed during the competition mesocycle. The last heavy workout on the clean and jerk and the snatch should be performed 10-14 days out, and squats should be dropped from the workouts approximately 14 days out.

Some suggestions for exercises to include in this mesocycle, by exercise category (see chapter six for exercise categories) are listed below:

Snatch exercises: Classic snatch, power snatch.

Snatch combination exercises: Classic snatch + overhead squats, snatch pulls + classic snatch.

Clean and jerk exercises: Classic clean, power clean, split jerk.

Clean and jerk combination exercises: Classic clean + split jerk.

Squats: Front squats and back squats.

Pulls: Snatch pulls (from the floor and from blocks), clean pulls (from the floor and from blocks).

Workouts for the competition mesocycle should be broken down as follows:

Day One: Snatch exercise, pulls, squats
Day Two: Clean and jerk exercise, pulls, squats
Day Three: Snatch combination exercise, pulls, squats
Day Four: Clean and jerk combination exercise, pulls, squats
Day Five: Snatch exercise, clean and jerk exercise

Hopefully, this chapter has given the reader an idea of what goes into designing a periodized training program for a beginning weightlifter. The chapter is meant to demonstrate certain concepts by taking the reader through the example, the chapter is not meant to be a program for every lifter - as every lifter is different and requires individualization.

References:

1. Ermakov, A.D., M.S. Abramyan, & V.F. Kim. (1980). The training load of weightlifters in pulls and squats. In Lelikov, S.I., A.S. Medvedev, Y.S. Povetkin, P.A. Poletayev, R.A. Roman, Y.A. Sandalov, & A.V. Chernyak (Eds.). 1980 Weightlifting Yearbook (pp. 34-38). Moscow: Fizkultura I Sport. Translated by Charniga, Jr., A. (1986). Livonia, Michigan: Sportivny Press. *Interesting ideas on the use of pulls and squats during the competition phase, also notes that pull and squat use should increase with a lifter's qualification.*

2. Frolov, V.I., & A.A. Lukashev. (1978). A comparative analysis of snatch and clean technique. Tyazhelaya Atletika, 26-28. Translated by Yesis, M. (1979). Soviet Sports Review, 14(2), 80-82. *This article seeks to hammer home the fact that the snatch and clean are performed differently, so they should be trained on different days.*

3. Laputin, N.P., & V.G. Oleshko. (1982). Managing the Training of Weightlifters. Kiev: Zdorov'ya Publishers. Translated by Charniga, Jr., A. Livonia, Michigan: Sportivny Press. *Another good book to provide information on how to organize long-term training plans.*

4. Medvedev, A.S. (1980). Periodization of training in weightlifting (The plan of preparation for a base meso-cycle). In Lelikov, S.I., A.S. Medvedev, Y.S. Povetkin, P.A. Poletayev, R.A. Roman, Y.A. Sandalov, & A.V. Chernyak (Eds.). 1980 Weightlifting Yearbook (pp. 16-25). Moscow: Fizkultura I Sport. Translated by Charniga, Jr., A. (1986). Livonia, Michigan: Sportivny Press. *Suggestions for set and rep schemes. Medvedev is very big on the performance of pulls and novel combination exercises.*

5. Medvedev, A.S. (1981). Training in the competition stage. In Lelikov, S.I., A.S. Medvedev, Y.S. Povetkin, P.A. Poletayev, R.A. Roman, Y.A. Sandalov, & A.V. Chernyak (Eds.). <u>1981 Weightlifting Yearbook</u> (pp. 27-32). Moscow: Fizkultura I Sport. Translated by Charniga, Jr., A. Livonia, Michigan: Sportivny Press. *Suggestions for set and rep schemes. Medvedev is very big on the performance of pulls and novel combination exercises.*

6. Medvedyev, A.S. (1986). <u>A System of Multi-Year Training in Weightlifting.</u> Moscow: Fizkultura I Sport. Translated by Charniga, Jr., A. (1989). Livonia, Michigan: Sportivny Press. *In my opinion, this one is a must read. Very detailed information on how to organize long-term training.*

7. Medvedyev, A.S. (1986). <u>A Program of Multi-Year Training in Weightlifting.</u> Moscow: Fizkultura I Sport. Translated by Charniga, Jr., A. (1995). Livonia, Michigan: Sportivny Press. *The companion volume to #6. Lays out the long-term training programs, over a period of years, for lifters of different classifications.*

8. Roman, R.A. (1986). <u>The Training of the Weightlifter.</u> Moscow: Fizkultura I Sport. Translated by Charniga, Jr., A. Livonia, Michigan: Sportivny Press. *Another must read. Roman and Medvedyev disagree on certain things, like the importance of pulls. Interested parties should read both and make their own decisions.*

Chapter Eight
Program Design for Intermediates

Chapter Outline:

What is an intermediate?
How the training year is broken down
The First Macrocycle
  Transitional Mesocycle
  General Preparation Mesocycle
  Special Preparation Mesocycle
  Competition Mesocycles

The Second Macrocycle
The Third Macrocycle
  Transitional Mesocycle
  General Preparation Mesocycle
  Special Preparation Mesocycle
  Competition Mesocycles

Chapter Objectives:

1. Understand what goes into the designing of programs for intermediates
2. Understand how to organize training into macrocycles and mesocycles
3. Understand how to manipulate exercise selection, volume, and intensity in each mesocycle

In this book, an intermediate lifter is defined as one who has qualified for a national-level event (for example, the American Open or Nationals). For an intermediate lifter, the focus of their training is to place (or win) at the national-level events.

There are a number of differences with their training. First, the overall volume of work will be greater. Second, the amount of work they do on snatches/cleans/jerks (relative to the total NL) will be greater than a beginner. Finally, intermediate lifters are training at a percentage of their 1-RM, as their technique should have stabilized enough to give them consistent 1-RM's.

The intermediate's training is still organized around three macrocycles: the first macrocycle runs from the day after Nationals through the Collegiate Nationals. The second macrocycle runs from the day after the Collegiate Nationals through the American Open. The third runs from the day after the American Open through Nationals. For purposes of this book we will use the 1997/1998 competition calendar. The lengths of the macrocycles are in table 8-1.

Macrocycle	Start Date	End Date	Length (weeks)
First	28 April 1997	11 Oct 1997	24
Second	12 Oct 1997	9 Nov 1997	4
Second	10 Nov 1997	6 April 1998	21

Table 8-1: Macrocycle Lengths for Beginners

The following sections will discuss in general how the macrocycles / mesocycles are organized and will go into detail on each of the macrocycles; explain how exercise selection, volume, and intensity should be manipulated.

The First Macrocycle

The first macrocycle runs from 21 April 1997 through the Collegiate Nationals, which ends on 11 October 1997. It lasts a total of 24 weeks. This macrocycle is broken down exactly as it was in chapter seven.

The entire breakdown of the first macrocycle can be seen in table 8-2.

Mesocycle	Start Date	End Date	Length (weeks)
Transitional	28 April 1997	10 May 1997	2
General Preparation	11 May 1997	21 June 1997	6
Developmental Meet	21 June 1997		
Special Preparation	22 June 1997	16 August 1997	8
Competition I	17 August 1997	30 August 1997	2
Prepatory Meet	30 August 1997		
Competition II	31 August 1997	11 October 1997	6
National Collegiates	11 October 1997		

Table 8-2: First macrocycle breakdown

The Transitional Mesocycle

Recall that the purpose of the transitional mesocycle is to allow the lifter a chance to recover from the previous macrocycle's training. This is achieved by a reduction in volume and intensity as well as a focus away from the competition movements. Lifters should not train more than six times during this two week mesocycle. Some suggestions for exercises to include in this mesocycle, by exercise category (see chapter six for exercise categories) are listed below:

Snatch exercises: Power snatch.

Snatch combination exercises: No exercises from this category.

Clean and Jerk exercises: Power clean.

Clean and Jerk combination exercises: No exercises from this category.

Squats: Back squats and front squats.

Pulls: No exercises from this category.

Bend Overs: Hyperextensions.

Presses: Military press (seated).

This means a total of 6 exercises are planned for the transitional mesocycle. Workouts should be broken down as follows:

> Workout One: Snatch, squats, GT
> Workout Two: Clean, squats, GT
> Workout Three: GT, bend overs, presses

Table 8-3 describes the set, rep, and average RI scheme for the exercises in this phase of training.

Exercise Category	Sets / Exercise	Reps / Set	Average RI
Snatch	3	4	50-60%
Clean and Jerk	3	4	50-60%
Squats	3	10	50-60%
Bend Overs	3	6	50-60%
Presses	3	6	50-60%

Table 8-3: Set and rep breakdown by exercise category for the transitional phase of the first macrocycle.

In the transitional phase, not only are the sets and reps reduced to make the workouts easy, but the exercises available for training are restricted to give the lifter a chance for some variety. The idea is to maintain motor skills while giving the lifter a chance to recover from hard training.

General Preparation Mesocycle

The purpose of the general preparation mesocycle is to develop the lifter's fitness. This is achieved by using a wide variety of exercises with a moderate amount of volume and intensity. Lifters will train 4 days per week in this phase. So this mesocycle will have a total of 24 workouts. The competition movements (classic snatch, classic clean) are performed every 3rd workout, as are combination lifts. The focus of this cycle is on "power" movements (i.e. power snatch/clean, etc.). This is to help the lifter develop the speed and explosiveness they need to improve on their competition lifts. In addition, pulls from the hang are also introduced in this part of the lifter's training. GT is performed once per week, as a result squats are only performed 3 times/week.

Some things to note about this phase and all the phases to be described in this chapter:
1. With squats, pulls, bend overs, and presses only work out sets are shown - i.e. warm up sets are not included when calculating NL or RI.
2. Pulls are performed with 10% more weight than the fundamental lifts (i.e. if you snatch at 70% then you perform pulls with 80%).

Workouts should be broken down, by week, as follows:

> Day One: Snatch exercises, pulls, front squats, bend overs
> Day Two: Clean and jerk exercises, pulls, back squats, presses
> Day Three: Snatch exercises, pulls, front squats
> Day Four: Clean and jerk exercises, pulls, GT

Table 8-4 describes the set, rep, and RI scheme for the exercises in this phase of training.

Exercise Category	Sets / Exercise	Reps / Set	Relative Intensity
Snatch exercises	5-6	3	70-85%
Snatch combination exercises	4-5	1-3	70-85%
Clean and Jerk exercises	6-7	3	70-85%
Clean and Jerk combination exercises	5-6	1-3	70-85%
Squats	3	4-6	70-85%
Pulls	3-4	2-4	80-95%
Bend Overs	3	4-6	NA
Presses	3	4-6	NA

Table 8-4: Set and rep breakdown by exercise category for the general preparation phase of the first macrocycle.

Some suggestions for exercises to include in this mesocycle, by exercise category are listed below.

Snatch exercises: Classic snatch, power snatch, power snatch from blocks (above and below the knee), overhead squats.

Snatch combination exercises: Power snatch + overhead squats (from the floor, from blocks), classic snatch + overhead squats

Clean and jerk exercises: Classic clean, power clean, power clean from blocks (above and below the knee), push jerks, split jerks.

Clean and jerk combination exercises: Power clean + split jerk (from the floor, from blocks), classic clean + split jerk.

Squats: Front squats, back squats.

Pulls: Snatch pulls (from the floor), snatch pulls from blocks (above and below the knee), snatch pulls from the hang (above and below the knee), clean pulls (from the floor), clean pulls from blocks (above and below the knee), clean pulls from the hang (above and below the knee).

Presses: Military press (standing), military press (seated), behind the neck press (snatch grip).

Bend Overs: Good mornings (standing), good mornings (seated), Romanian deadlifts.

A total of 37 exercises are planned for the general preparation mesocycle. A sample workout for the cycle follows:

Week One:
Workout #1:
1. Classic snatch   5x3x70%
2. Snatch pulls   4x4x80%
3. Front squats   3x6x70%
4. Good mornings, standing   3x6

Workout #2:
1. Split jerk   6x3x70%
2. Clean pulls   4x4x80%
3. Back squats   3x6x70%
4. Military press, standing   3x6

Workout #3:
1. Power snatch   5x3x70%
2. Snatch pulls, b, AK   3x4x80%
3. Front squats   3x6x70%

Workout #4:
1. Classic clean   6x3x70%
2. Clean pulls, b, AK   3x4x80%
3. GT

Total NL Week One: 194
Average RI Week One: 73.18%

Week Two:
Workout #5:
1. Power snatch, b, AK + Overhead squats
          1x3+2x70%, 3x3+2x75%
2. Snatch pulls, b, BK   4x3x85%
3. Front squats   3x4x75%
4. Good mornings, seated   3x6

Workout #6:
1. Power clean + Split jerk
          2x3+2x70%, 3x3+2x75%
2. Clean Pulls, b, BK   4x3x85%
3. Back squats   3x4x75%
4. Military press, seated   3x6

Workout #7:
1. Classic snatch   2x3x70%, 4x3x75%
2. Snatch pulls, h, AK   3x3x85%
3. Front Squats   3x6x75%

Workout #8:
1. Power clean, b, AK   3x3x70%, 4x3x75%
2. Clean pulls, h, AK   3x3x85%
3. GT

Total NL Week Two: 204
Average RI Week Two: 76.61%

Week Three:
Workout #9:
1. Overhead squats   1x3x70%,
   1x3x75%, 3x3x80%
2. Snatch pulls, h, BK 4x2x90%
3. Front squats   3x5x80%
4. Romanian deadlifts 3x5

Workout #10:
1. Classic clean   1x3x70%,
   2x3x75%, 4x3x80%
2. Clean pulls, h, BK   4x2x90%
3. Back squats   3x5x80%
4. Behind the neck press, snatch   3x5

Workout #11:
1. Power snatch + Overhead squats
          1x3+2x70%, 1x3+2x75%,
2x2+1x80%
2. Snatch pulls   3x2x90%
3. Front squats   3x5x80%

Workout #12:
1. Power clean, b, BK + Split jerk
          1x3+2x70%, 1x3+2x75%,
   3x2+1x80%
2. Clean pulls   3x2x90%
3. GT

Total NL Week Three: 174
Average RI Week Three: 80.17%

Week Four:
Workout #13:
1. Classic snatch   1x3x70%,
   1x3x75%, 3x3x80%
2. Snatch pulls, b, AK 4x2x90%
3. Front squats   3x5x80%
4. Good mornings, standing   3x5

Workout #14:
1. Push jerk   1x3x70%,
   3x3x75%, 2x3x80%
2. Clean pulls, b, AK   4x2x90%
3. Back squats   3x5x80%
4. Military press, standing   3x5

Workout #15:
1. Power snatch, b, AK   1x3x70%,
   1x3x75%, 3x3x80%
2. Snatch pulls, b, BK   4x2x90%
3. Front squats   3x5x80%

Workout #16:
1. Classic clean   1x3x70%,
   2x3x75%, 4x3x80%
2. Clean pulls, b, BK   4x2x90%
3. GT

Total NL Week Four: 176
Average RI Week Four: 80.65%

To prepare for the special preparation phase, starting with week 5 combination work will be performed every other workout.

Week Five:
Workout #17:
1. Power snatch, b, BK + Overhead squats
    1x3+2x70%, 1x3+2x75%,
    2x2+1x80%
2. Snatch pulls, h, AK   3x2x90%
3. Front squats   3x5x80%
4. Good mornings, seated   3x5

Workout #18:
1. Power clean + Split jerk
    1x3+2x70%, 2x3+2x75%,
    3x2+1x80%
2. Clean pulls, h, AK   3x2x90%
3. Back squats   3x5x80%
4. Military press, seated   3x5

Workout #19:
1. Classic snatch   1x3x70%,
    1x3x75%, 3x3x80%
2. Snatch pulls, h, BK   4x2x90%
3. Front squats   3x5x80%

Workout #20:
1. Power clean, b, AK   1x3x70%,
    1x3x75%, 4x3x80%
2. Clean pulls, h, BK   4x2x90%
3. GT

Total NL Week Five: 176
Average RI Week Five: 80.10%

Week Six:
Workout #21:
1. Power Snatch + Overhead squats
    1x3+2x70%, 1x3+2x77.5%,
    3x2+1x85%
2. Snatch pulls   3x2x95%
3. Front squats   3x4x85%
4. Romanian deadlifts 3x4

Workout #22:
1. Classic clean + Split jerk
    1x3+2x70%, 1x3+2x75%,
    1x2+1x80%, 3x2+1x85%
2. Clean pulls   3x2x95%
3. Back squats   3x4x85%
4. Behind the neck press, snatch   3x4

Workout #23:
Off

Workout #24:
Developmental meet

Total NL Week Six: 101
Average RI Week Six: 83.28%

Total NL general preparation mesocycle:
1025
Average RI general preparation mesocycle:
77.58%

Table 8-5 shows the breakdown of NL and average RI by the major exercises for the general preparation mesocycle described above.

Exercise Category	Total NL	% of Total NL	Average RI
Snatch exercises	179	17.5%	75.01%
Clean and jerk exercises	225	22%	74.98%
Squats	255	24.9%	77.53%
Pulls	198	19.3%	86.41%
Bend Overs	93	9.1%	NA
Presses	93	9.1%	NA

Table 8-5: Percentage of total NL for general preparation mesocycle, based on the workouts shown in text.

Special Preparation Mesocycle:

The purpose of the special preparation mesocycle is to apply the lifter's fitness to weightlifting. More work is spent developing technique and speed-strength. As a result, the competition lifts are emphasized while some of the assistance work is minimized in comparison. Volume and intensity are increased on the snatch, clean and jerk, squats, and pulls while it is maintained or reduced on the bend overs and presses. In this phase of the first macrocycle, lifters will train five times per week. Two workouts will be geared to the snatch, two to the clean and jerk, and one will train the snatch and the clean and jerk. Combination work is performed every other workout. GT is performed once every other week.

Some suggestions for exercises to include in this mesocycle, by exercise category are listed below:

Snatch exercises: Classic snatch, classic snatch from blocks (above and below the knee), power snatch, snatch balance.

Snatch combination exercises: Power snatch + overhead squats, classic snatch + overhead squats (from the floor, from blocks), pulls + classic snatch (from the floor, from blocks).

Clean and jerk exercises: Classic clean, classic clean from blocks (above and below the knee), power clean, squat jerks, split jerks.

Clean and jerk combination exercises: Power clean + split jerk, classic clean + split jerk (from the floor, from blocks).

Squats: Front squats, back squats.

Pulls: Snatch pulls (from the floor), snatch pulls from blocks (above and below the knee), snatch pulls from the hang (above and below the knee), clean pulls (from the floor), clean pulls from blocks (above and below the knee), clean pulls from the hang (above and below the knee).

Presses: Military press (standing), push press (jerk grip), push press (snatch grip)

Bend Overs: Good mornings (standing), good mornings (seated), good mornings (floor), Romanian deadlifts.

A total of 42 exercises are planned for the special preparation mesocycle. Workouts should be broken down as follows:

Day One: Snatch exercises, pulls, front squats, bend overs
Day Two: Clean and jerk exercises, pulls, back squats, presses
Day Three: Snatch exercises, pulls, front squats
Day Four: Clean and jerk exercises, pulls, back squats (or GT every other week)
Day Five: Snatch exercises, clean and jerk exercises

Table 8-6 describes the set and rep scheme for the exercises in this phase of training.

Exercise Category	Sets / Exercise	Reps / Set	Relative Intensity
Snatch Exercises	4-7	1-3	80-90%
Snatch Combination Exercises	4-8	1-3	80-90%
Clean and Jerk Exercises	5-9	1-3	80-90%
Clean and Jerk Combination Exercises	4-9	1-3	80-90%
Squats	3	2-5	80-90%
Pulls	3-4	2	90-100%
Bend Overs	3	2-5	NA
Presses	3	2-5	NA

Table 8-6: Set and rep breakdown by exercise category for the special preparation phase of the first macrocycle.

A sample workout for the special preparation phase follows, NL and average RI is included for each week.

<u>Week One:</u>
Workout #1:
1. Classic snatch   1x3x70%, 1x3x75%, 3x3x80%
2. Snatch pulls   4x2x90%
3. Front squats   3x5x80%
4. Good mornings, standing   3x5

Workout #2:
1. Split jerk   1x3x70%, 2x3x75%, 3x3x80%
2. Clean pulls   4x2x90%
3. Back squats   3x5x80%
4. Military press   3x5

Workout #3:
1. Classic snatch, b, AK + Overhead squats   1x3+2x70%, 1x3+2x75%, 3x2+1x80%
2. Snatch pulls, b, AK   3x2x90%
3. Front squats   3x4x80%

Workout #4:
1. Classic clean + Split jerk   1x3+2x70%, 2x3+2x75%, 4x2+1x80%
2. Clean pulls, b, AK   3x2x90%
3. Back squats   3x4x80%

Workout #5:
1. Classic snatch, b, BK   1x3x70%, 1x3x75%, 3x3x80%
2. Classic clean, b, AK   1x3x70%, 1x3x75%, 4x3x80%

Total NL Week One: 224
Average RI Week One: 79.54%

<u>Week Two:</u>
Workout #6:
1. Power snatch + Overhead squats   1x3+2x70%, 1x3+2x77.5%, 3x2+1x82.5%
2. Snatch pulls, b, BK   3x2x92.5%
3. Front squats   3x4x82.5%
4. Good mornings (seated)   3x4

Workout #7:
1. Classic clean, b, BK + Split jerk   1x3+2x70%, 2x3+2x77.5%, 3x2+1x82.5%
2. Clean pulls, b, BK   3x2x92.5%
3. Back squats   3x4x82.5%
4. Push press (jerk)   3x4

Workout #8:
1. Snatch balance   1x3x72.5%, 1x3x77.5%, 2x3x82.5%
2. Snatch pulls, h, AK   4x2x92.5%
3. Front squats   3x5x82.5%

Workout #9:
1. Power clean   1x3x72.5%, 1x3x77.5%, 3x3x82.5%
2. Clean pulls, h, AK   4x2x92.5%
3. GT

Workout #10:
1. Snatch pulls + Classic snatch   1x3+2x70%, 1x3+2x77.5%, 2x2+1x82.5%
2. Classic clean + Split jerk   1x3+2x70%, 1x3+2x77.5%, 3x2+1x82.5%

Total NL Week Two: 196
Average RI Week Two: 81.42%

<u>Week Three:</u>
Workout #11:
1. Classic snatch, b, AK   1x3x72.5%, 1x3x77.5%, 3x3x82.5%
2. Snatch pulls, h, BK   4x2x92.5%
3. Front squats   3x5x82.5%
4. Good mornings (floor)   3x5

Workout #12:
1. Squat jerk   1x3x72.5%, 2x3x77.5%, 2x3x82.5%
2. Clean pull, h, BK   4x2x92.5%
3. Back squats   3x5x82.5%
4. Push press (snatch)   3x5

Workout #13:
1. Classic snatch, b, BK + Overhead squats 1x3+2x70%, 1x3+2x77.5%, 3x2+1x82.5%
2. Snatch pulls 3x2x92.5%
3. Front squats 3x4x82.5%

Workout #14:
1. Classic clean + Split jerk 1x3+2x70%, 1x3+2x77.5%, 4x2+1x82.5%
2. Clean pulls 3x2x92.5%
3. Back squats 3x4x82.5%

Workout #15:
1. Power snatch 1x3x72.5%, 1x3x77.5%, 3x3x82.5%
2. Classic clean, b, AK 1x3x72.5%, 1x3x77.5%, 4x3x82.5%

Total NL Week Three: 216
Average RI Week Three: 82.02%

Week Four:
Workout #16:
1. Snatch pulls + Classic snatch 1x3+2x70%, 1x3+2x75%, 2x2+1x80%, 2x2+1x85%
2. Front squats 3x3x85%
3. Romanian deadlifts 3x3

Workout #17:
1. Classic clean, b, BK + Split jerk 1x3+2x70%, 1x3+2x75%, 2x2+1x80%, 3x2+1x85%
2. Clean pulls, b, AK 3x2x95%
3. Back squats 3x3x85%
4. Military press 3x3

Workout #18:
1. Snatch balance 1x3x70%, 1x3x75%, 2x3x80%, 2x2x85%
2. Snatch pulls, b, AK 4x2x95%
3. Front squats 3x4x85%

Workout #19:
1. Power clean 1x3x70%, 1x3x75%, 2x3x80%, 3x2x85%
2. Clean pulls, b, BK 4x2x95%
3. GT

Workout #20:
1. Classic snatch + Overhead squats 1x3+2x70%, 1x3+2x75%, 2x2+1x80%, 2x2+1x85%
2. Classic clean + Split jerk 1x3+2x70%, 1x3+2x75%, 2x2+1x80%, 3x2+1x85%

Total NL Week Four: 198
Average RI Week Four: 81.47%

Week Five:
Workout #21:
1. Classic snatch, b, AK 1x3x70%, 1x3x75%, 2x3x80%, 3x2x85%
2. Snatch pulls, b, BK 4x2x95%
3. Front squats 3x4x85%
4. Good mornings, standing 3x4

Workout #22:
1. Squat jerk 1x3x70%, 1x3x75%, 2x3x80%, 4x2x85%
2. Clean pulls, h, AK 4x2x95%
3. Back squats 3x4x85%
4. Push press (jerk) 3x4

Workout #23:
1. Snatch pulls, b, BK + Classic snatch, b, BK 1x3+2x70%, 1x3+2x75%, 2x2+1x80%, 3x2+1x85%
2. Front squats 3x3x85%

Workout #24:
1. Classic clean + Split jerk 1x3+2x70%, 1x3+2x75%, 2x2+1x80%, 4x2+1x85%
2. Clean pulls, h, BK 3x2x95%
3. Back squats 3x3x85%

Workout #25:
1. Power snatch 1x3x70%, 1x3x75%, 2x3x80%, 3x2x85%
2. Classic clean, b, AK 1x3x70%, 1x3x75%, 2x3x80%, 4x2x85%

Total NL Week Five: 217
Average RI Week Five: 78.39%

Week Six:
Workout #26:
1. Classic snatch + Overhead squats
      1x3+2x70%, 1x3+2x75%,
   2x2+1x80%, 4x2+1x85%
2. Snatch pulls, h, BK 3x2x95%
3. Front squats   3x3x85%
4. Good mornings, seated   3x3

Workout #27:
1. Classic clean, b, BK + Split jerk
      1x3+2x70%, 1x3+2x75%,
   2x2+1x80%, 5x2+1x85%
2. Clean pulls   3x2x95%
3. Back squats   3x3x85%
4. Push press (snatch)   3x3

Workout #28:
1. Snatch balance   1x3x70%,
   1x3x75%, 2x3x80%, 3x2x85%
2. Snatch pulls   4x2x95%
3. Front squats   3x4x85%

Workout #29:
1. Power clean   1x3x70%,
   1x3x75%, 2x3x80%, 4x2x85%
2. Clean pulls, b, AK   4x2x95%
3. GT

Workout #30:
1. Classic snatch + Overhead squats
      1x3+2x70%, 1x3+2x75%,
   2x2+1x80%, 4x2+1x85%
2. Classic clean + Split jerk
      1x3+2x70%, 1x3+2x75%,
   2x2+1x80%, 5x2+1x85%

Total NL Week Six: 232
Average RI Week Six: 82.43%

Week Seven:
Workout #31:
1. Classic snatch, b, AK   1x3x70%,
   2x2x80%, 2x1x85%, 2x1x90%
2. Snatch pulls, b, AK   3x2x100%
3. Front squats   3x2x90%
4. Good mornings (floor)   3x2

Workout #32:
1. Squat jerk   1x3x70%,
   2x2x80%, 3x1x85%, 3x1x90%
2. Clean Pulls, b, BK   3x2x100%
3. Back squats   3x2x90%
4. Military press   3x2

Workout #33:
1. Snatch pulls, b, BK + Classic snatch, b,
   BK 1x3+2x70%, 2x2+1x80%,
   2x2+1x85%, 2x1+1x90%
2. Front squats   3x2x90%

Workout #34:
1. Classic clean + Split jerk
      1x3+2x70%, 2x2+1x80%,
   2x2+1x85%, 3x1+1x90%
2. Back squats   3x2x90%

Workout #35:
1. Power snatch   1x3x70%,
   2x2x80%, 2x1x85%, 2x1x90%
2. Classic clean, b, AK   1x3x70%,
   2x2x80%, 2x1x85%, 3x1x90%

Total NL Week Seven: 139
Average RI Week Seven: 80.64%

Week Eight:
Workout #36:
1. Classic snatch + Overhead squats
      1x3+2x70%, 1x3+2x77.5%,
   4x2+1x82.5%
2. Snatch pulls, h, AK 3x3x92.5%
3. Front squats   3x4x82.5%
4. Romanian deadlifts 3x4

Workout #37:
1. Classic clean, b, BK + Split jerk
      1x3+2x70%, 2x3+2x77.5%,
   5x2+1x82.5%
2. Clean pulls, h, BK   3x3x92.5%
3. Back squats   3x4x82.5%
4. Push press (jerk)   3x4

Workout #38:
Off

Workout #39:
Off

Workout #40:
Prepatory meet

Total NL Week Eight: 118
Average RI Week Eight: 82.29%

Total NL for special preparation mesocycle:
1540
Average RI for special preparation
mesocycle: 80.96%

Table 8-7 shows the breakdown of NL for the major exercises for the workout described above.

Exercise Category	Total NL	% of Total NL	Average RI
Snatch exercises	352	22.9%	78.59%
Clean and Jerk exercises	476	30.9%	78.41%
Squats	282	18.3%	82.53%
Pulls	239	15.5%	88.19%
Bend Overs	90	5.8%	NA
Presses	90	5.8%	NA

Table 8-7: Percentage of total NL for special preparation mesocycle, based on the workout shown in text.

Competition Mesocycle:

The competition mesocycle is designed to bring everything together to allow the athlete to lift their best during competition. This phase of training sees the largest intensity, with a reduction in volume when compared to the other mesocycles. Assistance work is scaled back, the amount of time spent on snatches, clean and jerks, squats, and pulls is increased. During this mesocycle the athlete will be training six times a week (except for the week before competition, when the athlete will perform two workouts). The last heavy workout on the snatch should be performed no later than 7-9 days before competition, and the last heavy clean and jerk workout should be performed no later than 10-14 days before competition. GT is removed from training during this mesocycle.

Some suggestions for exercises to include in this mesocycle, by exercise category (see chapter six for exercise categories) are listed below:

Snatch exercises: Classic snatch, power snatch.

Snatch combination exercises: Power snatch + overhead squats, classic snatch + overhead squats, pulls + classic snatch.

Clean and jerk exercises: Classic clean, power clean, split jerks.

Clean and jerk combination exercises: Power clean + split jerk, classic clean + split jerk.

Squats: Front squats, back squats.

Pulls: Snatch pulls (from the floor), clean pulls (from the floor).

Presses: Push press (jerk grip), push press (snatch grip)

Bend Overs: Good mornings (standing), Romanian deadlifts.

A total of 18 exercises are planned for the competition mesocycle. Workouts should be broken down, by week, as follows:

Day One/Four: Snatch exercises, pulls, back squats, bend overs (once every other week)
Day Two/Five: Clean and jerk exercises, pulls, front squats, presses (once every other week)
Day Three/Six: Snatch exercises, clean and jerk exercises

Table 8-8 describes the set and rep scheme for the exercises in this phase of training.

Exercise Category	Sets / Exercise	Reps / Set	Relative Intensity
Snatch Exercises	3-9	1-3	85-95%
Snatch Combination Exercises	3-9	1-3	85-95%
Clean and Jerk Exercises	3-9	1-3	85-95%
Clean and Jerk Combination Exercises	3-10	1-3	85-95%
Squats	3	1-3	85-95%
Pulls	3-4	1-3	95-105%
Bend Overs	3	2-3	NA
Presses	3	2-3	NA

Table 8-8: Set and rep breakdown by exercise category for the competition phase of the first macrocycle.

A sample workout for the competition I and competition II phases follows.

Competition I

Week One:
Workout #1:
1. Classic snatch   1x3x70, 1x3x80, 2x2x85, 3x1x90
2. Snatch pulls   3x2x100
3. Back squats   3x2x90
4. Good mornings, standing   3x2

Workout #2:
1. Classic clean + Split jerk   1x3+2x70, 1x3+2x80, 2x2+1x85, 4x1+1x90
2. Clean pulls   3x2x100
3. Front squats   3x2x90
4. Push press (jerk)   3x2

Workout #3:
1. Power snatch + Overhead squats   1x3+2x70, 1x2+1x80, 2x2+1x85, 3x1+1x90
2. Classic clean   1x3x70, 1x3x80, 2x2x85, 4x1x90

Workout #4:
1. Classic snatch   1x3x70, 1x3x80, 2x2x85, 3x1x90
2. Snatch pulls   3x2x100
3. Back squats   3x2x90

Workout #5:
1. Power clean + Split jerk   1x3+2x70, 1x3+2x80, 2x2+1x85, 4x1+1x90
2. Clean pulls   3x2x100
3. Front squats   3x2x90

Workout #6:
1. Classic snatch + Overhead squats   1x3+2x70, 1x2+1x80, 2x2+1x85, 3x1+1x90
2. Classic clean   1x3x70, 1x3x80, 2x2x85, 4x1x90

Total NL Week One: 202
Average RI Week One: 85.37%

Week Two:
Workout #7:
1. Power snatch   1x3x70, 2x2x80, 3x1x85
2. Snatch pulls   4x2x95
3. Back squats   3x2x85

Workout #8:
1. Power clean   1x3x70, 2x2x80, 4x1x85
2. Clean pulls   4x2x95
3. Front squats   3x2x85

Workout #9-11:
Off

Workout #12:
Collegiate Nationals

Total NL Week Two: 49
Average RI Week Two: 85.61%

Competition II

Week Three:
Workout #13:
1. Classic snatch   1x3x70, 2x2x80, 3x2x85
2. Snatch pulls   4x2x95
3. Back squats   3x3x85
4. Romanian deadlifts   3x3

Workout #14:
1. Classic clean + Split jerk   1x3+2x70, 2x2+1x80, 4x2+1x85
2. Clean pulls   3x2x95
3. Front squats   3x2x85
4. Push press (snatch)   3x3

Workout #15:
1. Classic snatch + Overhead squats 1x3+2x70, 2x2+1x80, 3x2+1x85
2. Power clean   1x3x70, 2x2x80, 4x2x85

Workout #16:
1. Power snatch   1x3x70, 2x2x80, 3x2x85
2. Snatch pulls   4x2x95
3. Back squats   3x3x85

Workout #17:
1. Classic clean + Split jerk   1x3+2x70, 2x2+1x80, 4x2+1x85
2. Clean pulls   3x2x95
3. Front squats   3x2x85

Workout #18:
1. Classic snatch + Overhead squats 1x3+2x70, 2x2+1x80, 3x2+1x85
2. Classic clean 1x3x70, 2x2x80, 4x2x85

Total NL Week Three: 218
Average RI Week Three: 83%

Week Four:
Workout #19:
1. Classic snatch   1x3x70, 1x3x80, 2x2x85, 2x1x90, 2x1x95
2. Snatch pulls   3x1x105
3. Back squats   3x1x95

Workout #20:
1. Power clean + Split jerk   1x3+2x70, 1x2+1x80, 2x2+1x85, 2x1+1x90, 3x1+1x95
2. Clean pulls   3x1x105
3. Front squats   3x1x95

Workout #21:
1. Power snatch + Overhead squats 1x3+2x70, 1x2+1x80, 2x1+1x85, 2x1+1x90, 2x1+1x95
2. Classic clean   1x3x70, 1x3x80, 2x2x85, 2x1x90, 3x1x95

Workout #22:
1. Classic snatch   1x3x70, 1x3x80, 2x2x85, 2x1x90, 2x1x95
2. Snatch pulls   4x1x105
3. Back squats   3x1x95

Workout #23:
1. Classic clean + Split jerk   1x3+2x70, 1x2+1x80, 2x2+1x85, 2x1+1x90, 3x1+1x95
2. Clean pulls   3x1x105
3. Front squats   3x1x95

Workout #24:
1. Classic snatch + Overhead squats 1x3+2x70, 1x2+1x80, 2x1+1x85, 2x1+1x90, 2x1+1x95
2. Power clean   1x3x70, 1x3x80, 2x2x85, 2x1x90, 3x1x95

Total NL Week Four: 171
Average RI Week Four: 86.17%

Starting with week five, squats and other assistance work (except pulls) are dropped from the program.

Week Five:
Workout #25:
1. Power snatch   1x3x70, 1x3x80, 2x2x85, 2x1x90, 3x1x95
2. Snatch pulls   4x1x105

Workout #26:
1. Classic clean + Split jerk   1x3+2x70, 1x2+1x80, 2x2+1x85, 2x1+1x90, 4x1+1x95
2. Clean pulls   3x1x105

Workout #27:
1. Classic snatch + Overhead squats
        1x3+2x70, 1x2+1x80, 2x1+1x85,
        2x1+1x90, 3x1+1x95
2. Classic clean   1x3x70, 1x3x80,
        2x2x85, 2x1x90, 4x1x95

Workout #28:
1. Classic snatch   3x3x70
2. Snatch pulls   3x3x70

Workout #29:
1. Power clean + Split jerk   3x3+2x70
2. Clean pulls   3x3x70

Workout #30:
1. Power snatch + Overhead squats
        3x3+2x70
2. Classic clean   3x3x70

Total NL Week Five: 152

Average RI Week Five: 79.21%

Week Six:
Workout #31:
1. Classic snatch   3x3x70
2. Snatch pulls   3x3x70

Workout #32:
1. Power clean + Split jerk   3x3+2x70
2. Clean pulls   3x3x70

Workouts #33-35:
Off

Workout #36:
American Open

Total NL Week Six: 42
Average RI Week Six: 70%

Total NL competition mesocycle: 834
Average RI competition mesocycle: 83%

Table 8-9 shows the breakdown of NL and average RI for the major exercises for the competition phase described above.

Exercise Category	Total NL	% of Total NL	Average RI
Snatch exercises	267	32%	84.42%
Clean and Jerk exercises	293	35%	89.15%
Squats	78	9.4%	88.08%
Pulls	124	14.9%	90.32%
Bend Overs	15	1.8%	NA
Presses	15	1.8%	NA

Table 8-9: Percentage of total NL for competition mesocycles, based on the workout shown in text.

Figure 8-1 shows the NL and intensity for each week described in the text above.

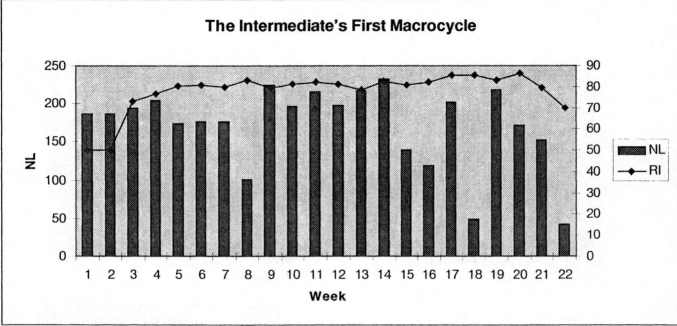

Figure 8-1: NL distribution by week for the first macrocycle, through competition II.

The Second Macrocycle

The second macrocycle is designed to peak the lifter for the American Open (7-9 Nov 1997). This meet is only four weeks after Collegiate Nationals which presents programming difficulties for a coach. The goal here is to improve the lifter's total while avoiding overtraining after the peaking process for Collegiate Nationals. As a result, the lifter's training will be broken down as follows:

Day One: Snatch exercises, snatch pulls, squats, bend overs (every 2nd week)
Day Two: Clean and jerk exercises, clean pulls, squats, presses (every 2nd week)
Day Three: Snatch exercises, clean and jerk exercises
Day Four: Snatch exercises, snatch pulls, squats
Day Five: Clean + Jerk, clean pulls, squats
Day Six: Snatch exercises, clean and jerk exercises

Lifters will employ exercises from the following categories. Notice that with the exception of the clean + jerk, combination exercises are removed from the program:

Snatch exercises: Classic snatch and power snatch.

Clean and jerk exercises: Classic clean and power clean.

Clean and jerk combination exercises: Classic clean + split jerk.

Pulls: Snatch and clean pulls from the floor.

Squats: Front and back squats.

Presses: Military press.

Bend Overs: Good mornings, standing.

A total of 11 exercises are planned for this macrocycle of training.

With this training cycle, there isn't time to include a transitional phase. The first week of training (i.e. the week after Collegiate's) should be a reduced week - 3 sets/exercise with lighter weights (around 85% or 1-RM). Weeks two and three should have an increased loading (i.e. 95% of 1-RM) with heavy weights. Week four (week of American Open) should only include 2-3 workouts with lighter weights (70% of 1-RM).

The Third Macrocycle

This macrocycle is designed to peak the lifter for Nationals. The breakdown for this cycle can be seen in table 8-10.

Mesocycle	Start Date	End Date	Length (weeks)
Transitional I	10 November 1997	23 November 1997	2
Transitional II	24 November 1997	7 December 1997	2
General Preparation	8 December 1997	17 January 1998	6
Developmental Meet	17 January 1998		
Special Preparation	18 January 1998	21 February 1998	5
Prepatory Meet	21 February 1998		
Competition	22 February 1998	6 April 1998	6
Nationals	4-6 April 1998		

Table 8-10: Breakdown of the third macrocycle.

Transitional Mesocycles:
This training beings after the lifter has competed in the American Open. The lifter has completed 28 rigorous weeks of training without any real down time. For this period of training, there are two different transitional mesocycles. The first one emphasizes general training to provide variety and expand the lifter's fitness; the second one gets the lifter back to performing the competition lifts.

Transitional I Mesocycle:
This mesocycle is designed to keep the lifter training, teach them new skills, and keep the lifter out of the weight room to allow for recovery. This phase emphasizes GT. Squats are eliminated from the program during the transitional I mesocycle.

In addition to GT, lifters will perform exercises from the following categories:

Bend overs: Hyperextensions, good mornings (standing).

Presses: Military press, behind the neck press (snatch grip).

During this mesocycle, training will be broken down as follows:

```
Day One:   GT, bend overs
Day Two:   GT, presses
Day Three: GT
```

As with all transitional phases, volume and intensity are low - lifters should perform 3 sets of 4 reps/exercise with very light and easy weights.

Transitional II Mesocycle:

This cycle continues to promote active recovery and begins to get the lifter used to training the Olympic lifts. Squats and the Olympic lifts are gradually integrated with the GT starting with this phase.

Lifters will employ exercises from the following categories during this phase of training:

Snatch exercises: Power snatch.

Clean and Jerk exercises: Power clean, push jerk.

Squats: Front squats, back squats.

Bend overs: Hyperextensions, good mornings (standing).

Presses: Military press, behind the neck press (snatch grip).

A total of 9 exercises are planned for the transitional II mesocycle. Workouts are broken down as follows:

Day One: Snatch exercises, squats, GT
Day Two: Clean and jerk exercises, squats, GT
Day Three: GT, bend overs, presses

Once again, volume is kept to 3 sets/exercise, with 4 reps/ set. The weights should be light and easy (the focus should be on technique).

General Preparation Mesocycle:

This phase lasts 6 weeks. As before, the idea is to develop the lifter's all-around fitness. Lifters will train 5 days/week, with 2 GT sessions integrated each week. This is done to continue to develop speed and explosiveness. It also provides variety. The competition movements are performed every 3rd workout, however the focus is on "power" movements (i.e. power snatch, power clean, etc.). In addition, combination lifts are only performed every 3rd workout. The sets and reps break down like in table 8-4. Movements from the hang are introduced into the lifter's training with this cycle (i.e. hang snatch, hang clean). In addition the exercises available in the pulls category are expanded to include pulls from 4 stops.

Some suggestions for exercises to include in this mesocycle, by exercise category (see chapter six for exercise categories) are listed below:

Snatch exercises: Classic snatch, power snatch, power snatch from the hang (above and below the knee), overhead squats.

Snatch combination exercises: Power snatch + overhead squats (from the floor, from the hang), classic snatch + overhead squats

Clean and jerk exercises: Classic clean, power clean, power clean from the hang (above and below the knee), push jerks, split jerks.

Clean and jerk combination exercises: Power clean + split jerk (from the floor, from the hang), classic clean + split jerk.

Squats: Front squats, back squats.

Pulls: Snatch pulls (from the floor), snatch pulls from the hang (above and below the knee), snatch pulls in 4 positions (from AK + from knee + from BK + from floor), clean pulls (from the floor), clean pulls from the hang (above and below the knee), clean pulls in 4 positions (from AK + knee + from BK + from floor).

Presses: Military press (standing), military press (seated), behind the neck press (snatch grip).

Bend Overs: Good mornings (standing), good mornings (seated), Romanian deadlifts.

Workouts for the general preparation mesocycle should be broken down as follows:

Day One: Snatch exercise, pulls, front squats
Day Two: Clean and jerk exercises, pulls, back squats
Day Three: GT, bend overs, presses
Day Four: Snatch exercises, pulls, front squats
Day Five: Clean and jerk exercises, pulls, GT

Special Preparation Mesocycle:

This phase lasts 5 weeks and still seeks to apply the lifter's fitness to the sport of Olympic lifting. Lifters will train 6 days/week during this phase. Once again, speed movements are introduced and the competition lifts are prioritized as assistance work is gradually phased out. GT is integrated with the weight workouts, although it is only performed three times per two week period. Also note that day six is a two-a-day. For set and rep suggestions, see table 8-6.

Some suggestions for exercises to include in this mesocycle, by exercise category (see chapter six for exercise categories) are listed below:

Snatch exercises: Classic snatch, classic snatch from the hang (above and below the knee), power snatch, snatch balance.

Snatch combination exercises: Power snatch + overhead squats, classic snatch + overhead squats (from the floor, from the hang), pulls + classic snatch (from the floor, from the hang).

Clean and jerk exercises: Classic clean, classic clean from the hang (above and below the knee), power clean, squat jerks, split jerks.

Clean and jerk combination exercises: Power clean + split jerk, classic clean + split jerk (from the floor, from the hang).

Squats: Front squats, back squats.

Pulls: Snatch pulls (from the floor), snatch pulls from the hang (above and below the knee), snatch pulls from 4 positions, snatch pulls from plinths, clean pulls (from the floor), clean pulls from the hang (above and below the knee), clean pulls from 4 positions, clean pulls from plinths.

Presses: Military press (standing), push press (jerk grip), push press (snatch grip)

Bend Overs: Good mornings (standing), good mornings (seated), good mornings (floor), Romanian deadlifts.

Workouts for the special preparation mesocycle should be broken down as follows:

> Day One: Snatch exercises, pulls, front squats
> Day Two: Clean and jerk exercises, pulls, back squats
> Day Three: GT, bend overs
> Day Four: Snatch exercises, pulls, front squats
> Day Five: Clean and jerk exercises, pulls, back squats
> Day Six: AM: GT, presses (GT every other week), PM: Snatch exercises, clean and jerk
>   exercises

Competition Mesocycle:

This phase lasts 6 weeks and is designed to peak the lifter for Nationals. Except for the week of Nationals, lifters will train 6 days/week. For set and rep suggestions, see table 8-8. GT is removed from the lifter's training, to allow more focus on the competition lifts. In addition, assistance work is almost completely phased out unless it is needed - presses and bend overs are not performed during the competition mesocycle. The last heavy workout on the clean and jerk and the snatch should be performed 10-14 days out, and squats should be dropped from the workouts approximately 14 days out.

Some suggestions for exercises to include in this mesocycle, by exercise category (see chapter six for exercise categories) are listed below:

Snatch exercises: Classic snatch, power snatch.

Snatch combination exercises: Power snatch + overhead squats, classic snatch + overhead squats, pulls + classic snatch.

Clean and jerk exercises: Classic clean, power clean, split jerks.

Clean and jerk combination exercises: Power clean + split jerk, classic clean + split jerk.

Squats: Front squats, back squats.

Pulls: Snatch pulls (from the floor), clean pulls (from the floor).

Workouts for the competition mesocycle should be broken down as follows:

> Day One: Snatch exercises, pulls
> Day Two: Clean and jerk exercises, pulls, back squats
> Day Three: Snatch exercises, clean and jerk exercises
> Day Four: Snatch exercises, pulls, front squats
> Day Five: Clean and jerk exercises, pulls, back squats
> Day Six: Snatch exercises, clean and jerk exercises

References:

1. Ermakov, A.D., M.S. Abramyan, & V.F. Kim. (1980). The training load of weightlifters in pulls and squats. In Lelikov, S.I., A.S. Medvedev, Y.S. Povetkin, P.A. Poletayev, R.A. Roman, Y.A. Sandalov, & A.V. Chernyak (Eds.). <u>1980 Weightlifting Yearbook</u> (pp. 34-38). Moscow: Fizkultura I Sport. Translated by Charniga, Jr., A. (1986). Livonia, Michigan: Sportivny Press. *Interesting ideas on the use of pulls and squats during the competition phase, also notes that pull and squat use should increase with a lifter's qualification.*

2. Frolov, V.I., & A.A. Lukashev. (1978). A comparative analysis of snatch and clean technique. <u>Tyazhelaya Atletika,</u> 26-28. Translated by Yesis, M. (1979). <u>Soviet Sports Review, 14</u>(2), 80-82. *This article seeks to hammer home the fact that the snatch and clean are performed differently, so they should be trained on different days.*

3. Laputin, N.P., & V.G. Oleshko. (1982). <u>Managing the Training of Weightlifters.</u> Kiev: Zdorov'ya Publishers. Translated by Charniga, Jr., A. Livonia, Michigan: Sportivny Press. *Another good book to provide information on how to organize long-term training plans.*

4. Medvedev, A.S. (1980). Periodization of training in weightlifting (The plan of preparation for a base meso-cycle). In Lelikov, S.I., A.S. Medvedev, Y.S. Povetkin, P.A. Poletayev, R.A. Roman, Y.A. Sandalov, & A.V. Chernyak (Eds.). <u>1980 Weightlifting Yearbook</u> (pp. 16-25). Moscow: Fizkultura I Sport. Translated by Charniga, Jr., A. (1986). Livonia, Michigan: Sportivny Press. *Suggestions for set and rep schemes. Medvedev is very big on the performance of pulls and novel combination exercises.*

5. Medvedev, A.S. (1981). Training in the competition stage. In Lelikov, S.I., A.S. Medvedev, Y.S. Povetkin, P.A. Poletayev, R.A. Roman, Y.A. Sandalov, & A.V. Chernyak (Eds.). <u>1981 Weightlifting Yearbook</u> (pp. 27-32). Moscow: Fizkultura I Sport. Translated by Charniga, Jr., A. Livonia, Michigan: Sportivny Press. *Suggestions for set and rep schemes. Medvedev is very big on the performance of pulls and novel combination exercises.*

6. Medvedyev, A.S. (1986). <u>A System of Multi-Year Training in Weightlifting.</u> Moscow: Fizkultura I Sport. Translated by Charniga, Jr., A. (1989). Livonia, Michigan: Sportivny Press. *In my opinion, this one is a must read. Very detailed information on how to organize long-term training.*

7. Medvedyev, A.S. (1986). <u>A Program of Multi-Year Training in Weightlifting.</u> Moscow: Fizkultura I Sport. Translated by Charniga, Jr., A. (1995). Livonia, Michigan: Sportivny Press. *The companion volume to #6. Lays out the long-term training programs, over a period of years, for lifters of different classifications.*

8. Roman, R.A. (1986). <u>The Training of the Weightlifter.</u> Moscow: Fizkultura I Sport. Translated by Charniga, Jr., A. Livonia, Michigan: Sportivny Press. *Another must read. Roman and Medvedyev disagree on certain things, like the importance of pulls. Interested parties should read both and make their own decisions.*

PART THREE: COMMON ERRORS

This section is divided into three chapters, one dealing with the clean, one with the jerk, and one with the snatch. This is not meant to be a comprehensive look at every error possible, just some of the most common ones (in my experience).

Chapter Nine
Common Errors with the Clean

Chapter Outline:

Starting Position Errors:
  Rounded back
  "Squatting" into position during the hang
  clean
  Hips too high in the start
Pull Errors
  Hitting the knees or shins
  Throwing the bar away from the body

Bending the arms excessively
Hips traveling faster than shoulders
Receiving Errors
  Elbows touching the knees
  Failure to "land" on flat feet
  Lifter falls backwards
  Losing control of the bar
  Splitting the feet to the sides excessively

Chapter Outline:

1. Become familiar with some of the more common errors during the clean.
2. Understand what causes these errors and how they can be treated.

Starting Position Errors

Rounded Back

This is a frequent problem with beginners. Sometimes this can be caused simply by poor technique, in other cases it can be caused by a lack of flexibility. The starting position, with the stomach between the legs and the torso upright is an uncomfortable one for many - particularly those with poor lower back development. Performing the deadlift with a clean grip can be a good exercise to help reinforce proper starting technique.

In some cases lifters may not be aware they are doing this. If that is true, then the coach should stand next to the lifter and place on hand on the lifter's upper chest and one hand on the small of the lifter's back. The coach should then push back on the chest and push in on the back until the lifter is in the proper position (1).

"Squatting" into position during the hang clean instead of bending forward

Many beginning lifters are taught that this is okay. While this position is not incorrect, it is inefficient. When allowed to squat into position the muscles that extend the knees will be the ones to primarily power the clean. When forced to bend from the hips, the muscles that act on the hips will be the ones to primarily power the clean. Those muscles that act on the hips are larger and more powerful than those that act on the knees. In other words, by "squatting" into position one limits how powerful and explosive they can be on these lifts.

Lifter has their hips too high in the starting position

This is a problem because when the lifter's hips are too high at the start, this can result in them slamming the bar into their knees or shins when pulling it off the ground. The coach should stand next to the lifter, place one hand on their upper chest and place the other hand on the small of the lifter's back. From there the coach should push the lifter's hips down into the proper position (1) (see photo 9-1).

Photo 9-1: Lifter's hips are too high during the start.

Pull Errors

Hitting the knees or shins

As beginners are learning the coordination they need to perform these lifts they may slam the bar into their knees or shins during the first pull. This is a coordination problem. It is usually caused by the lifter trying to force the bar back towards the body during the pull or by performing the first pull too quickly. Another cause of this may be due to the lifter having their shoulders too far in front of the bar (i.e. their hips are too high relative to their knees) (1, 3).

If the lifter extends their knees during the first pull, the bar will move back towards the body on its own. A possible solution to performing the pull too quickly is to have the lifter practice the deadlift with a clean grip (i.e. lift the bar from the floor to mid-thigh).

Throwing the bar away from the body

The farther away from the body the bar is, the harder the bar is to control (i.e. the exercise becomes more difficult). Usually this is caused by the lifter not paying attention to their technique and it can also be caused by bending the elbows during the first and second pulls. Also, some lifters will bounce the bar off their thighs during the pull and try to "curl" the weight instead of dropping under it. Performing cleans from the hang or from blocks can be used to remedy this.

Photo 9-2: Bending the arms excessively during the pull.

Bending the arms excessively

The arms need to remain straight throughout the first and second pulls. When the elbows are allowed to bend that means that the biceps power the pulls. Because the biceps are a great deal smaller and weaker than the muscles of the lower body and back this will cause the lifter to pull the bar more slowly.

In other words, by bending the elbows during the pulls the entire lift will slow down - making it more difficult to perform (see photo 9-2).

Once again, cleans from the hang or from blocks can be used to remedy this - usually these exercises are hard enough that one has to learn to be properly explosive to perform them successfully. Another coaching cue that can be used to solve this problem is by insuring that the lifter has their elbows rotated out during the pull - this makes it more difficult bend the elbows (1).

Photo 9-3: Lifter's hips are traveling faster than their shoulders.

Hips traveling faster than the shoulders
This can be caused by a number of things; general poor technique, too much weight on the bar, or pulling too quickly from the floor (see photo 9-3) (3). A good remedy for this problem is to perform the deadlift with a clean grip (1).

Receiving Errors

Elbows touching the knees
This is grounds for a disqualification of the lift. This error has a couple of possible causes; poor lower back strength, an incomplete pull - i.e. the lifter moves under the bar too quickly, and jumping backwards. Front squats, good mornings, cleans from the hang, and clean pulls can all be performed to aid this (2).

Failure to "land" on flat feet
This is dangerous because the lifter is off-balance. It is usually caused by splitting the feet to the sides, by jumping backwards during the clean, or by poor ankle flexibility (1). When lifters are allowed to get into this habit, it guarantees that they will have trouble learning the classic clean because it is difficult to receive the bar in a full squat when one lands on their toes.

Lifter falls backwards during the clean
This is dangerous because the lifter is off-balance. It can result from leaning backwards too far during the pull, from swinging the bar away from the body, or from swinging the bar and jumping forward to meet it. Pulls and cleans from the hang are a good way to work on this problem (2).

Losing control of the bar
This is the result of any of a multitude of errors during the first and second pulls. If the bar is thrown away from the body during the pulls, the lifter will be off-balance when they catch the bar. If the back is not set, or if the elbows are not kept high, the lifter will not be able to control the bar when catching it. If the second pull is too slow, or if the bar is not pulled to a great enough height, the lifter will be off balance when racking the bar. In addition, some lifters will jump too far forward or backwards and this will put them off-balance when catching the bar. Many missed lifts are due to a lack of back strength (i.e. when the lifter receives the bar they slump forward, losing control). Front squats aid greatly in learning to keep control of the bar in a deep clean.

Photo 9-4: Splitting the feet to the sides excessively during the clean.

Splitting the feet to the sides excessively
Once again, many lifters are taught that this is okay. However, this is potentially very dangerous as it increases the amount of strain placed on the knee joints. In addition, if lifters are taught to split their feet to the sides they tend to exaggerate this motion whenever the weights get heavy (see photo 9-4).

References

1. (1987). The United States Weightlifting Federation Coaching Manual Volume I: Technique (pp. 76-87). Baker, G. (Ed.) Colorado Springs, CO: United States Weightlifting Federation.
2. Jones, L. (1991). USWF Coaching Accreditation Course Senior Coach Manual. Colorado Springs, CO.: United States Weightlifting Federation, 113-119.
3. Laputin, N.P., & V.G. Oleshko. (1982). Managing the Training of Weightlifters. Kiev: Zdorov'ya Publishers. Translated by Charniga, Jr. A. Livonia, Michigan: Sportivny Press, 80-93.

Chapter Ten
Common Errors during the Jerk

Chapter Outline:

Errors during the dip and drive
 Hitting the chin
 Bar doesn't move with the lifter during dip
 Slow transition between dip and drive
 Dipping from the knees
Errors during the split

Being off balance
Failure to catch the bar on locked elbows
Unlocking the elbows are catching the bar
Failure to split the feet far enough apart
Looking down during the jerk
Errors during the recovery
 Moving the wrong foot first

Chapter Objectives:

1. Be familiar with some of the more common errors associated with the jerk
2. Understand what causes some of these errors

Errors during the dip and drive

Hitting the chin during the lift
This error is somewhat rare. However when it does happen it is usually from one of two things: first, the lifter may not be paying attention to what they are doing. One should always remember where their head is during this exercise. Second, the lifter could be driving backwards instead of straight up (1). When this happens, and the bar misses the lifter's chin, it results in the bar being too far behind the lifter when they are in the split - so the lifter is off balance. The push jerk can be used to train this problem.

Bar doesn't move with the lifter during the dip
When this happens, the lifter dips down but the bar doesn't travel with the lifter - it comes crashing down as the lifter begins the drive. Usually this can be fixed by calling the lifter's attention to the problem and by getting them to grip the bar more loosely during the dip (1).

Slow transition between dip and drive
Pausing at the bottom of the dip will limit the amount of force a lifter can generate in this lift (1, 3). Coaches should remind lifters that there is no pause in this part of the lift. Sometimes jumping exercises can help reinforce good technique (1).

Dipping from the knees and not the hips
A lifter should squat during the dip, which means the dip should be performed by pushing the hips back and down. The jerk should not be performed solely by bending the knees. First, this will limit the amount of force that can be produced. Second, it shifts the weight of the bar forward and puts the lifter off balance right at the start of the lift. Squat from the hips. Push jerks and front squats are excellent ways to train this.

Errors during the split

Being off balance when the bar is overhead

This is caused by the lifter not keeping the bar over the hips (1). If the bar is too far in front, or too far behind, the lifter will be off balance. It can be caused by a failure to keep the back set during the lift, by driving "backwards" instead of straight up (see above about hitting the chin), or by driving "forward" (2). Push jerks are an excellent way to train balance and dip/drive technique.

Failure to catch the bar with the elbows locked during the split jerk

This is a disqualification in the split jerk and could result from a number of things: a drive off the shoulders that is too slow, a dip and drive that is too weak, failure to split the feet far enough forward and back, failure to split the feet quickly enough, or from a poor arm lock (see photo 10-1). The lifter can perform push jerks to help develop this; also the coach should emphasize the need to split the feet quickly after the drive (2).

Photo 10-1: Failure to catch the bar with the arms locked out.

Bending the elbows after catching the bar

This is another disqualification in the split jerk and lifters should be trained not to do this when practicing the lift. This is frequently caused by "over-jerking" (i.e. jerking too hard). Lifters should be reminded to continually push against the bar to keep their arms locked out (1).

Failure to split the feet far enough

As mentioned before, this could lead to the elbows being bent when catching the bar. Usually this stems from a couple of things; lack of confidence (after all, dropping under a heavy barbell is not a natural act), poor technique, and also lack of flexibility.

Looking down during the jerk
When lifters look down while jerking, it tends to round the back somewhat and it moves the bar forward - throwing the lifter off balance. The head should be neutral during the jerk.

Errors during the recovery

Bringing the rear foot forward first during the recovery
The reason this is bad is that it throws the lifter off balance during the recovery. When the rear foot is brought forward first, it tends to throw the barbell forward which can lead to the lifter being off balance (1).

References

1. (1987). <u>The United States Weightlifting Federation Coaching Manual Volume I: Technique</u> (pp. 76-87). Baker, G. (Ed.) Colorado Springs, CO: United States Weightlifting Federation.
2. Jones, L. (1991). <u>USWF Coaching Accreditation Course Senior Coach Manual.</u> Colorado Springs, CO.: United States Weightlifting Federation, 113-119.
3. Laputin, N.P., & V.G. Oleshko. (1982). <u>Managing the Training of Weightlifters.</u> Kiev: Zdorov'ya Publishers. Translated by Charniga, Jr. A. Livonia, Michigan: Sportivny Press, 80-93.

Chapter Eleven
Common Errors during the Snatch

Chapter Outline:

Starting position errors
 Rounded back
 "Squatting" into position
Pull errors
 Hitting the knees
 Throwing the bar away from the body
 Bending the arms excessively

Hips traveling too fast
Receiving errors
 Splitting the feet
 Failure to land on flat feet
 Not catching with locked arms
 Bending the arms
 Losing control

Chapter Outline:

1. Be familiar with some of the common errors associated with the snatch
2. Understand what causes these errors and how they can be fixed

Starting Position Errors

Rounded Back
This is a frequent problem with beginners. Sometimes this can be caused simply by poor technique, in other cases it can be caused by a lack of flexibility. The starting position, with the stomach between the legs and the torso upright is an uncomfortable one for many - particularly those with poor lower back strength. Performing the deadlift with a snatch grip can be a good exercise to help reinforce proper starting technique.

In some cases lifters may not be aware they are doing this. If that is true, then the coach should stand next to the lifter and place one hand on the lifter's upper chest and one hand on the small of the lifter's back. The coach should then push back on the chest and push in on the back until the lifter is in the proper position (1).

"Squatting" into position during the hang clean instead of bending forward
Many beginning lifters are taught that this is okay. While this position is not incorrect, it is inefficient. When allowed to squat into position the muscles that extend the knees will be the ones to primarily power the snatch. When forced to bend from the hips, the muscles that act on the hips will be the ones to primarily power the snatch. Those muscles that act on the hips are larger and more powerful than those that act on the knees. In other words, by "squatting" into position one limits how powerful and explosive they can be on these lifts.

Lifter has their hips too high in the starting position
This is a problem because when the lifter's hips are too high at the start, this can result in them slamming the bar into their knees or shins when pulling it off the ground. The coach should stand next to the lifter, place one hand on their upper chest and place the other hand on the small of the lifter's back. From there the coach should push the lifter's hips down into the proper position (1) (see photo 9-1).

Pull Errors

Hitting the knees or shins

As beginners are learning the coordination they need to perform these lifts they may slam the bar into their knees or shins during the first pull. This is a coordination problem. It is usually caused by the lifter trying to force the bar back towards the body during the pull or by performing the first pull too quickly. Another cause of this may be due to the lifter having their shoulders too far in front of the bar (i.e. their hips are too high relative to their knees) (1, 3). If the lifter extends their knees during the first pull, the bar will move back towards the body on its own. A possible solution to performing the pull too quickly is to have the lifter practice the deadlift with a snatch grip (i.e. lift the bar from the floor to hip level).

Throwing the bar away from the body

The farther away from the body the bar is, the harder the bar is to control (i.e. the exercise becomes more difficult). Usually this is caused by the lifter not paying attention to their technique and it can also be caused by bending the elbows during the first and second pulls. Also, some lifters will bounce the bar off their hips during the pull and try to "lateral raise" the weight instead of dropping under it. Performing snatches from the hang or from blocks can be used to remedy this.

Bending the arms excessively

The arms need to remain straight throughout the first and second pulls. When the elbows are allowed to bend that means that the biceps muscles power the pulls. Because the biceps are a great deal smaller and weaker than the muscles of the lower body and back this will cause the lifter to pull the bar more slowly. In other words, by bending the elbows during the pulls the entire lift will slow down - making it more difficult to perform (see photo 9-2) (3, 4). Once again, snatches from the hang or from blocks can be used to remedy this - usually these exercises are hard enough that one has to learn to be properly explosive to perform them successfully. Another coaching cue that can be used to solve this problem is by insuring that the lifter has their elbows rotated out during the pull - this makes it more difficult for them to bend their elbows (1).

Hips traveling faster than the shoulders

This can be caused by a number of things: general poor technique, too much weight on the bar, or pulling too quickly from the floor (see photo 9-3) (3). A good remedy for this problem is to perform the deadlift with a snatch grip (1).

Receiving Position Errors

Splitting the feet to the side during hang or power snatches

Once again, many lifters are taught that this is okay. However, this is potentially very dangerous as it increases the amount of strain placed on the knee joints. In addition, if lifters are taught to split their feet to the sides they tend to exaggerate this motion whenever the weight gets heavy.

Failure to "land" on flat feet

This is dangerous because the lifter is off-balance. It is usually caused by splitting the feet to the sides or by jumping backwards during the snatch. When lifters are allowed to get into this habit, it guarantees that they will have trouble learning the classic snatch because it is difficult to receive the bar in a full squat when one lands on their toes.

Failure to catch the bar with locked out arms during the snatch

This can be due to several things. First, the lifter may not be paying attention to their technique. Second, the lifter may not be pulling the bar high enough. Finally, the lifter may not be moving under the bar fast enough. Lifters should spend some time working on pulls/snatches from the hang and from blocks to develop their speed (2). In competition, if the bar is not caught with the elbows locked out it will disqualify the attempt (see photo 11-1).

Photo 11-1: Failure to catch the bar with the arms locked out.

Bending the elbows after catching the bar

This will disqualify the lift. The elbows must remain locked out from the catch until the bar is released.

Losing control of the bar after catching it

This can be the result of a multitude of errors. The bar may have been thrown away from the body during the first and second pulls, causing the lifter to catch the bar too far back. The lifter may not have pulled the bar to a great enough height, making control difficult during the squat under. The elbows may have been bent during the catch, making it difficult to control the bar. The bar may have been caught in a position that is not over the hips, putting the lifter off balance. In addition, the lifter may have jumped forward or backwards to meet the bar (2).

References

1. (1987). <u>The United States Weightlifting Federation Coaching Manual Volume I: Technique</u> (pp. 76-87). Baker, G. (Ed.) Colorado Springs, CO: United States Weightlifting Federation.
2. Jones, L. (1991). <u>USWF Coaching Accreditation Course Senior Coach Manual.</u> Colorado Springs, CO.: United States Weightlifting Federation, 113-119.
3. Laputin, N.P., & V.G. Oleshko. (1982). <u>Managing the Training of Weightlifters.</u> Kiev: Zdorov'ya Publishers. Translated by Charniga, Jr. A. Livonia, Michigan: Sportivny Press, 80-93.
4. Lukashev, A.A., & Melkonyan, A.A. (1980). Substantiation of methods of perfecting snatch technique of class II weightlifters. In Lelikov, S.I., A.S. Medvedev, Y.S. Povetkin, P.A. Poletayev, R.A. Roman, Y.A. Sandalov, & A.V. Chernyak (Eds.). <u>1980 Weightlifting Yearbook</u> (pp. 46-55). Moscow: Fizkultura I Sport. Translated by Charniga, Jr., A. (1986). Livonia, Michigan: Sportivny Press.

Appendix A
Weight Classes and IWF Competition Rules

Weight Classes

Olympic-style weightlifting is an Olympic sport for both men and women. Women will compete in the Olympics for the first time during the 2000 Games. There are ten weight classes for men and eight weight classes for women:

Weight Class (kg)	Weight Class (lbs)
under 47	under 103.4
51	112.2
56	123.2
62	136.4
69	151.8
77	169.4
85	187
94	206.8
105	231
105+	231+

Table A-1: Weight Classes for Men

Weight Class (kg)	Weight Class (lbs)
under 43	94.6
48	105.6
53	116.6
58	127.6
63	138.6
69	151.8
75	165
75+	165+

Table A-2: Weight Classes for Women

IWF COMPETITION RULES

2.1 The Snatch

2.1.1. The barbell is placed horizontally in front of the lifter's legs. It is gripped, palms downwards and pulled in a single movement from the platform to the full extent of both arms above the head, while either splitting or bending the legs. During this continuous movement, the bar may slide along the thighs and the lap. No part of the body other than the feet may touch the platform during the execution of the lift. The weight which has been lifted must be maintained in the final motionless position, arms and legs extended, the feet in the same line, until the referees give the signal to replace the barbell on the platform. The turning over of the wrists must not take place until the bar has passed the top of the lifter's head. The lifter may recover in his own time, either from a split or a squat position, and have his feet on the same line, parallel to the planes of the trunk and the barbell. The referees give the signal to lower the barbell as soon as the lifter becomes motionless in all parts of the body.

2.2 The Clean and Jerk

2.2.1 The first part, the Clean:

The bar is placed horizontally in front of the lifter's legs. It is gripped, palms downward and pulled in a single movement from the platform to the shoulders, while either splitting or bending the legs. During this continuous movement, the bar may slide along the thighs and the lap. The bar must not touch the chest before the final position. It then rests on the clavicles or on the chest above the nipples or on the arms fully bent. The feet return to the same line, legs straight, before performing the Jerk. The lifter may make this recovery in his own time and have his feet on the same line, parallel to the plane of his trunk and the barbell.

2.2.2 The second part, the Jerk:
The athlete bends the legs and extends them as well as the arms to bring the bar to the full stretch of the arms vertically extended. He returns the feet to the same line, arms and legs extended and waits for the referees' signal to replace the bar on the platform. The referees give the signal to lower the barbell as soon as the lifter becomes motionless in all parts of the body.

Important Remark:
After the Clean and before the Jerk, the lifter may assure the position of the bar. This must not lead to confusion. It cannot mean in any case, granting an additional jerk attempt to the lifter, but allowing him to either:

    a) withdraw his thumbs or "unhook" if he is using this method,

    b) lower the bar in order to let it rest on his shoulders if the bar is placed too high and impedes his breathing or causes pain,

    c) change the width of the grip.

2.3 General Rules for All Lifts

2.3.1 The technique known as "hooking" is permitted. It consists of covering the last joint of the thumb with the other fingers of the same hand at the moment of gripping the bar.

2.3.2 In all lifts, the referees must count as "No lift" any unfinished attempt in which the bar has reached the height of the knees.

2.3.3 After the referees' signal to lower the barbell, the lifter must lower it in front of the body and not let it drop either deliberately or accidentally. He may release his grip on the bar when it has passed the level of his waist.

2.3.4 If a competitor cannot fully stretch his arm due to an anatomical deformation, he must report this fact to the three referees and the jury before the start of the competition.

2.3.5 When snatching or cleaning in the squat position, the lifter may help his recovery by swinging and rocking movements of his body.

2.3.6 The use of grease, oil, water, talcum or any similar lubricant on the thighs is forbidden. The lifter cannot have *any* substance on his/her legs when he/she arrives in the competition area. The lifter who uses a lubricant is ordered to remove it. During the removal the clock goes on. The use of chalk (magnesium) on the hands, thighs, etc. is permitted.

2.4 Incorrect Movements and Position for All Lifts

2.4.1 Pulling from the hang.

2.4.2 Touching the platform with any part of the body other than the feet.

2.4.3 Uneven or incomplete extension of the arms at the finish of the lift.

2.4.4 Pause during the extension of the arms.

2.4.5 Finishing with a press-out.

2.4.6 Bending and extending the arms during the recovery.

2.4.7 Leaving the platform during the execution of the lift, i.e. touching the area outside the platform with any part of the body.

2.4.8 Replacing the bar on the platform before the referees' signal.

2.4.9 Dropping the bar after the referees' signal (front or behind).

2.4.10 Failing to finish with the feet and the barbell in line and parallel to the plane of the trunk.

2.4.11 Failing to replace the complete barbell on the platform, i.e. the complete barbell must first touch the platform.

2.5 Incorrect Movements for The Snatch
2.5.1 Pause during the lifting of the bar.

2.5.2 Touching the head of the lifter with the bar when finishing the lift.

2.6 Incorrect Movements for The Clean
2.6.1 Placing the bar on the chest before turning the elbows.

2.6.2 Touching the thighs or the knees with the elbows or the upper arms.

2.7 Incorrect Movements for The Jerk
2.7.1 Any apparent effort of jerking which is not completed. This includes lowering the body or bending the knees.

2.7.2 Any deliberate oscillation of the barbell to gain advantage. The athlete and the barbell have to become motionless before starting the jerk.

(from United States Weightlifting Federation Official Rule Book 1994 Edition, United States Weightlifting Federation, Inc., Colorado Springs, CO, 54-56. Reprinted by permission of USA Weightlifting.)